Sacred Psychology
of Change

LIFE AS A VOYAGE
OF TRANSFORMATION

Sacred Psychology of Change

LIFE AS A VOYAGE
OF TRANSFORMATION

Marilyn C. Barrick, Ph.D.

SUMMIT UNIVERSITY 🕯 PRESS®

Gardiner, Montana

SACRED PSYCHOLOGY OF CHANGE
Life as a Voyage of Transformation
by Marilyn C. Barrick, Ph.D.

For information:
The Summit Lighthouse, 63 Summit Way, Gardiner, MT 59030 USA
1-800-245-5445 / 406-848-9500
TSLinfo@TSL.org
SummitLighthouse.org

Visit Dr. Barrick's web site at www.spiritualpsychology.com.

Cover painting: Roxanne Duke

Library of Congress Catalog Card Number: 99-69804
ISBN: 978-0-922729-57-9

SUMMIT UNIVERSITY 🦢 PRESS®

I dedicate this book to the hearts and souls
of people everywhere who are seeking
the joy and fulfillment of transformation
and renewal midst the turmoil
of changing times.

My prayer is that we may so transcend
ourselves in the new millennium that we
successfully complete our Voyage of Life
while we are loved and guided by angels
from the higher realms of Spirit.

May your inner hero and heroine's higher
vision, love and aspirations be as a lighthouse
to guide you through every stormy cycle of
change until you arrive safely Home.

Contents

Author's Prologue

As each of us welcomes the new millennium, we are called to become adepts at handling fast-moving change while remaining faithful to the inner mission of our heart and soul. Advances in our civilization also mandate understanding the new sciences and the increasingly complex technology needed to convey vast amounts of information that descend with lightning speed upon us every day.

In my thirty-five years of practice as a clinical psychologist and transformational therapist, I have seen many people, just like you and me, attempting to grapple with the issues of change and the accelerated pace of our times. In the past ten years, concern about these issues has increased exponentially as the whirlwind of change has reached the doorstep of more and more people.

People often tell me they are on information overload at work, at home and even during vacations. They describe their daily lives as impelled by an inner sense of running to catch up. They can't seem to keep up with the information flashing through the media, the newspapers, web sites and all kinds of communication devices. It's the same drama all over the world.

Throughout the globe we see big changes in cultural customs: ever-rising divorce rates, growing numbers of homeless or latchkey children, frequent ups and downs in the job markets and increasing financial constraints and disruption of family life due to job-mandated moves and corporate downsizing.

Families today find it difficult to get together for the holidays without it being a big deal, where it used to be that grandparents, parents and siblings lived within shouting distance of one another. With many grandparents no longer close to home, children are losing a transfer of life's wisdom that used to be commonplace.

In contrast to the early years of the twentieth century, life at the beginning of the twenty-first century is substantially more complicated. Our ever-expanding technological advances have impacted the ways we learn, the ways we communicate, the ways we interact with one another. The pace of change has stepped up tremendously as a result of worldwide media and computerized everything.

We are increasingly aware that we are more than simple townspeople, city folks or citizens of our country of birth. We are called to become citizens of the world. We can no longer ignore the necessity for cross-cultural exchange, worldwide information systems, international jet travel and space exploration—nor may we safely close our eyes and ears to threats of terrorism, modern nuclear devices and the potential for biological warfare.

Our modern civilization's preoccupation with technical achievement is also having a subtle but major impact on our inner world. High-tech multimedia presentations do not encourage the heart's reflection, intuitiveness and creativity. Today's movie, TV and video productions are such fast-paced, tumultuous and explicit extravaganzas that they leave little room for the viewer's imagination.

It is becoming a real challenge to maintain a sense of inner tranquillity and outer composure midst the whirl of activity and constant change in cultural mores, job expectations and life on the home front. Sometimes we feel a bit like Alice in Wonderland tumbling head over heels into a curious, upside-down world.

People tell me that when they think about all that is demanded of them every day, they feel tense, "wired," their minds running ahead of them and their bodies stressed. Sometimes they get totally maxed out and decide, "Well, I don't know what to do about all this. I'm overwhelmed. I'm going home for the day." But we can't go home for the day from life. It's still going to be here today, tomorrow and on into the future as long as we live on this earth.

What can we do when we feel overwhelmed and stressed out over everything going on in our lives? That's what this book is all about—and more!

Here are some beginning questions to ponder: Where is our world going in such haste? Is civility keeping pace with civilization? If not, what is happening to our soul and spirit?* What kind of destiny are we forging for our children and future generations? How can I make a difference?

---

*The soul, whether housed in a male or female body, is the feminine counterpart of Spirit; spirit [lowercase] means our masculine essence.

I have written *Sacred Psychology of Change: Life as a Voyage of Transformation* to share my thoughts and reflections as I have pondered these questions for myself and with my clients. I have had the opportunity to accompany many wonderful people on their inner transformational journey. I wanted to write this book to help all those whom I will never get to see and talk to, face to face.

My hope is that each of us will choose to greet the cycles of change in the new millennium as magnificent opportunities for transformational growth. My prayer is that we so accelerate our love and higher vision for one another that we fulfill our personal destiny and contribute to the victory of compassion and renewal on planet Earth.

Introduction

*Life is a river which flows through
many times and changes.*

—Anonymous

When I first saw the four beautiful masterpieces by the artist Thomas Cole depicting the voyage of life,[1] I realized that these paintings, reproduced in the center of this book, truly portray the essence of our life journey. In Cole's first painting, an infant is entering the waters of life in a boat piloted by an angel. His second painting shows the angel watching from the bank as the youth excitedly sets off on a voyage by himself. Cole's third painting depicts the man of middle age praying to God as his boat moves through rapids and shoals of very rough waters and angels watch from the clouds above. The fourth painting depicts angels guiding the boat as the old man returns home to God.

These beautiful works of art became a meditation for me. In a meditative state I saw them representing both the inner and outer voyage of life. The outer voyage moves through the stages as Cole named his paintings: *Childhood, Youth, Manhood* and *Old Age*.

My vision of the inner voyage of life is of the *soul's* journey through this lifetime or perhaps many lifetimes. I see the soul as the inner spiritual being of man or woman who moves from a state of innocence through dreams of youthful adventure to the forging of destiny in manhood or womanhood to the fruition of the soul's life work in the golden years.

I envision each of us as a son or daughter of God whose soul is imbued with a divine love spark meant to ignite love on the earth in some very special way. Each of us begins our journey of life with hopes and dreams and the excitement of many possibilities. We bring to earth from the heaven-world unique talents of soul and treasures of Spirit to develop and offer to others.

As each stage of life unfolds, we meet new people, changing circumstances and bountiful opportunities to learn, to grow and to give. I believe that our destiny on earth is to become the fullness of our God-created potential and to offer our special gifts to those we love and those we meet along life's way. Ultimately, we return home to the realms of Spirit, the heaven-world, having fulfilled our mission of love, which is unique for each one.

Offering love to the world means many different things. We may express our spark of love through the arts, the sciences, religion and spirituality, medicine, education, communication and information services, architecture, cultural advancement, environmental preservation—each one of us could add to the list.

One way or another we are meant to offer to the earth and her people that unique gift of love that is inherent in our soul. As children of Universal Love, the very essence of our being is divine love. And each of us has our own creative way of expressing love to our Maker and to loved ones, friends, acquaintances and strangers along the way. How? It's the simple things: a kind word, a creative idea, a helpful deed, a listening ear, a warmhearted response, a smile, a hug, a cheery hello, a word of appreciation.

Each day we make many decisions and take many actions. We might ask ourselves at the end of the day: Have my decisions and actions today been loving? If the answer is yes, we are on target. If the answer is no, we need to reset ourselves so that tomorrow we can say, "Yes!"

During our journey in time and space we have the help of our inner knight champion, our Higher Self (Christ Self or Buddha Self) who is meant to be our personal guide and mentor on this great voyage of life. We are in touch with our Higher Self when we feel the prick of conscience, the compassion of our heart, or when we respond to life from higher values. I dedicate this book on the sacred psychology of change to the reunion of our soul and Higher Self and to our transformational victory through the adventures of the inner and outer voyage of life.

CHAPTER ONE

Forging Our Destiny in a Changing World

Change is inevitable.
Growth is optional.

—JOHN MAXWELL

As the world watched the TV coverage of the airplane crash that took the lives of John F. Kennedy Jr., his wife Carolyn and her sister in 1999, many were reminded of the death of Princess Diana two years before and of Mother Teresa so close in time. What is it about these end-of-life dramas that captures the attention, the heart and soul of people all over the world?

Perhaps it is the uneasiness evoked by the seeming randomness of sudden tragedy and by the necessity of coming to grips with one's own mortality. The Kennedys and Princess Diana were so young—snuffed out in the springtime of life. Why? What does it mean? Perhaps it is more than a little scary. Could it happen to me? These are thoughts and feelings that people have shared with me.

In contrast, people seem to have more of a sense of peace about the death of Mother Teresa. She was in the winter of her life, somehow more ready to move on. She had realized her mission as a loving servant of God and sought to fulfill it every day. She left markings for others to follow. She brought love and comfort to the "poorest of the poor." Mourned but not lost, she lives on in the hearts of those she served.

We might say the same of Gandhi, Joan of Arc, Abraham Lincoln and Bernadette Soubirous of Lourdes. Each one suffered an early, or seemingly untimely death. Yet they live on in the legacy they left to us.

Some ask, Are these great figures of history alive and well in a higher realm? Will they have the opportunity to come to planet Earth again? Do people ever reincarnate? There are those who tell us they remember their previous lifetimes and whose convictions about it are unshakable. Others who have had near-death experiences speak of schools for the soul in higher realms. Some who have gone on have even been given the opportunity to communicate with those they have left behind.[1]

Those who believe they have lived before say that our lives are not judged in threescore and ten, but that we are granted many opportunities to fulfill our soul's destiny. Some believe that certain true teachings of the great adepts have been lost or disregarded, including their teachings about reembodiment for the continuing evolution of the soul.

A Lesson from the Bridge of San Luis Rey

Where is truth? Perhaps we have only begun to comprehend the vastness of the plan of the Creator for each one of us. Do you remember the historical tragedy of the bridge of San Luis Rey? Five people were flung to their deaths when that most famous bridge in Peru collapsed on July 10, 1714. Franciscan monk Brother Juniper and twentieth-century writer Thornton Wilder both wrote an answer to the question, "Why did it happen to those five?"

Brother Juniper's meticulously detailed research in the 1700s determined it to have been divine intervention rather than capricious fate. For all of his trouble, he and his book of research were declared heretical and publicly burned. Two hundred years later, from a dusty surviving copy of that work, Thornton Wilder captured the inner passion and meaning of the intertwined lives of those five people in his Pulitzer Prize winning book, *The Bridge of San Luis Rey.*

The Abbess Madre María's final words in Wilder's novel speak a great truth applicable to events of our time. She muses to herself, "Soon we shall die and all memory of those five will have left the earth, and we ourselves shall be loved for a while and forgotten. But the love will have been enough; all those impulses of love return to the love that made them. Even memory is not necessary for love. There is a land of the living and a land of the dead and the bridge is love, the only survival, the only meaning."[2]

Each of us must find our own answers to the inner questions that arise when the world mourns the sudden death of individuals who have touched the hearts and souls of many people. These are soul-searching questions. Why am I still here? What is the meaning of life? If my life were to end tomorrow, would I have fulfilled my purpose?

I believe that while we are alive and well here on earth we have a unique opportunity to explore, to forge and to fulfill a special destiny in our rapidly changing world. What is that destiny? It is individual for each one of us. Yet as Thornton Wilder concludes—it always has to do with how we live and how we love.

Spiritual Adepts as Cultural Change Agents

The Great Lights of the world's religions have set the tone for cultural change, personal transformation and the fulfillment of each soul's destiny. By fearless example and wise and gentle teachings, avatars, saints and sages have lived and taught the precepts of the heart as they healed the sick, comforted the afflicted, blessed the little children and offered to each one hope and renewed vision. They have offered their cultures a living example of holy purpose and love's destiny fulfilled.

Even as these adepts fulfilled their mission of divine love victoriously, they have prepared the way for each of us to do the same. As we move into the Aquarian age, we have the opportunity to offer our special gift of love to a world in the throes of change. Each one's gift, be it ever so humble, becomes a message of hope and reassurance to the soul that the consciousness of divine love transcends the human condition.

Lighting the Way in the Aquarian Age with a Spark of Divine Love

Saints and mystics such as Saint Francis and Clare, Ramakrishna, Mahatma Gandhi, Paramahansa Yogananda, Padre Pio and Mother Teresa followed in the wake of the adepts of old. As we trace their footprints, we, too, may light the way in the Aquarian age from the spark of divine love burning brightly in our hearts.

What does it mean to "light the way?" To me it means

to be true to ourselves and to our God, to stoke the love fires in our hearts, to offer gentle understanding and loving kindness to all, to extend a helping hand to the less fortunate.

It means to tap into the greatest healing power of the universe, the power of divine love as compassion, and to anchor that kindness and mercy in the earth through loving thoughts, words and deeds. Thus, we become living vessels to offer God's gift of compassion to all life. As we allow the waters of divine love to pour through our hearts to all we meet, we help quench the thirst of a planet and a people.

Mother Teresa showed us this miracle. She reached out to saints and sinners alike. She was equally compassionate with rich and poor, heads of governments and the man on the street, the healthy and the sick. Through her wise and loving heart, she crossed the barriers of human fear and hatred and uplifted everyone she met through selfless acts of loving kindness.

Malcolm Muggeridge writes of Mother Teresa, "It will be for posterity to decide whether she is a saint. I only say of her that in a dark time she is a burning and a shining light; in a cruel time, a living embodiment of Christ's gospel of love; in a godless time, the Word dwelling among us, full of grace and truth. For this, all who have the inestimable privilege of knowing her, or knowing of her, must be eternally grateful."[3]

I do believe she is a saint of our times who brought about a miracle of change in people's lives—change for the better, change from sickness to health, change from fear to peaceful acceptance. The light of divine love poured through her as she offered each one the tender care that emanated from her heart and soul and physical being.

As reporter Licia Corbella wrote in her December 1, 1996 article in *The Calgary Sunday Sun* after she had seen Mother Teresa arrive at the airport in Calgary:

"...I was particularly awed by the glow around her. The woman literally had a halo. I'm not joking. It was an aura similar to the light you can see shining around the heads of the saints or Jesus in old religious paintings."[4]

Mother Teresa was fond of handing out her "business cards," five short lines offering her science of compassion to those she met along the road of life:

The fruit of silence is *prayer.*
The fruit of prayer is *faith.*
The fruit of faith is *love.*
The fruit of love is *service.*
The fruit of service is *peace.*

Mother Teresa's footsteps still echo in the age of Aquarius, which astrologers and mystics tell us is foretold to be an age of divine love.[5]

Walking the Earth with Compassion

How may we become the loving, compassionate adepts that we are meant to be in the midst of whirling change? It isn't really a matter of how much time we spend with someone. It's more about how understanding and caring we are to others—and to ourselves.

Compassion means caring enough to walk in the moccasins of another for awhile and, through a loving understanding of that person's plight, to offer whatever help that one needs to move forward, one step at a time. As we learn to listen to the often unspoken request of the heart and soul of someone in need and to follow the gentle guidance of our own heart and soul, we intuitively come to know the common-sense next step and what we can do to help.

Poets, musicians and lovers have always spoken the language of the heart. We hold our children close to our hearts to soothe them. And on one special day each year, Valentine's Day, we send heart-to-heart messages of love to one another through gifts and special remembrances. Our attunement with our heart or the lack of it affects our own lives, the lives of our loved ones and everyone with whom we make contact.

Perhaps it is not so surprising that the new sciences are shedding light on how these precious experiences are associated with the heart and how the higher vibrations of our heart offer us intuitive wisdom and guidance when we take the time and space to quiet ourselves and listen.

The Heart as the Harmonizer of Cellular Activity

For a number of years, Doc Lew Childre and other dedicated scientists at the Institute of HeartMath in Boulder Creek, California, have been exploring how the heart, mind and body interact. Through EEG, EKG and other measurements taken while people focus on their hearts, their breathing and memories of positive feelings, these Aquarian explorers offer us a scientific motivation for becoming heart-centered.

Their work demonstrates that uplifting feelings such as joy, compassion, appreciation and humor not only reduce stress and produce a sense of calmness and peace but also correlate with "coherent," or harmonic, frequencies in the heart. By contrast, negative feelings such as worry, anxiety, frustration and hurt increase stress and correlate with "incoherent," or disorderly and chaotic, frequencies in the heart's electrical system.[6]

Entrainment Creates Physical, Emotional and Mental Harmony

What researchers at the Institute of HeartMath are describing as coherent frequencies of the heart correlate with higher aspects of human nature such as genuine caring, enlightened understanding, patience, loving kindness and the uplift that comes from just plain fun. Inner synchronicity, or what Doc Childre calls "entrainment"[7] of our internal systems, occurs as we focus our attention on the heart, the flow of the breath and uplifting feelings.

As the heart entrains the brain, the brain entrains the cells and the cells entrain the body systems, such as the immune system and the neurological system. Our physical, emotional and mental processes begin to work together efficiently and harmoniously. We feel centered, energized and positive.

Another discovery is that when we focus our attention

on the higher intelligence of our heart and look at the "up-side" of problematic situations, our sympathetic and para-sympathetic nervous systems work together in harmony. Our bodies are energized, our minds are alert and we are prepared for positive problem-solving and creative interaction with others.

On the other hand, when we get caught in the "down-side" and get stressed out, frustrated, fearful or angry, our sympathetic and parasympathetic systems essentially end up doing battle with each other. The result is a start-and-stop process, similar to putting on the gas and hitting the brake at almost the same time, which creates both physical and emotional distress.

The Enlightened Heart: Our Greatest Gift

On a spiritual level, when we become heart-centered, we broaden our perspective to the "big picture." We harmonize our thoughts, feelings and physical responses with our higher vision and sense of purpose. We may ask for and receive specific direction from God through our Higher Self. We validate for ourselves the mystical understanding that the enlightened heart is our greatest gift and the refined human brain is meant to be the good servant of the heart—rather than the other way around.

This understanding is perhaps one of the biggest keys to facing difficult or unexpected change. We must be in our hearts, not just our heads. For it is through the heart that we will receive God's guidance and reassurance.

In my own life, I have verified that the counsel of my Higher Self through my heart is accurate and correlates with my meditations and inner vision. In fact, this process initiated my writing career. When a twenty-year work cycle ended, I asked God through my heart for new direction. I received the answer in words of living fire in front of my eyes though they were closed: *Write down what thou hast received.*

I knew it was both a spiritual and practical direction. I realized I was to put on paper an integration of the spiritual and psychological truths I have gleaned from lifelong inner and outer experiences. As I do so, I am blessed with feelings of excitement, joy and peace.

Understanding Our Holographic Nature

Another important aspect of who we are and how we are meant to relate to life comes from understanding that we are holographic in nature. In a hologram, the pattern of the whole is complete in every part, even as each part serves as a portion of the whole. Thus, each element of the hologram mirrors the overall holographic pattern.

Our bodies are actually holographic. Every cell in the body contains the nucleus of what it would take to create another human body. We also resonate with one another, individually and collectively, as we share time and space and exchange energy.

Perhaps you have had the experience of "feeling" someone's attention on you from across the room. You notice it because when someone's attention is focused upon you, that person's energy travels to you over the arc of attention. Energetically, we connect with whomever and whatever we put our attention upon because wherever our attention is focused, our energy flows.

The more intimate the interaction, the more energy we exchange. We may begin to take on some of our friends' attitudes or mannerisms. It isn't just a matter of modeling ourselves after them; it has to do with the intertwining of our energies.

I remember when I understood this for the first time. I was working as a psychologist in a university counseling center and counseling many young people who were involved in intimate relationships. This was the sixties and seventies, and many of them were trying out sexual intimacy as a way of getting to know one another.

A number of the young women who came in for counseling were feeling very confused within themselves. They would say things like, "I don't feel like I'm the person I used to be before I started dating so much." Or "I feel like I have something going on inside of me that isn't me. And it's confusing."

I began to keep track of these young women because they were usually involved in multiple relationships, and I had a hunch that had something to do with their confusion. I soon verified that the girls who were sleeping around were the ones who seemed the most "mixed up" inside.

I asked several of these young women if they would be willing to abstain from sexual intimacy for a month and see if they noticed any change in how they felt about themselves. Each of them came back in a month reporting with some surprise and chagrin that they had a clearer sense of themselves again. One of them put my hypothesis into her own words: "I think I was taking on a lot from those guys, and I was getting myself scrambled up with them."

Our Heart as the Conductor of the Inner Symphony of Mind, Body and Spirit

We are learning from the fields of energy cardiology and cardiac psychology just how holographic we may be and how integral our hearts are to the process. The research of psychoneuroimmunologist Paul Pearsall, Ph.D. offers evidence that not only does the heart emit more electricity than the human brain, but it also functions as a central "harmonizer" of cellular activity.

Dr. Pearsall offers compelling evidence that "the heart conducts the cellular symphony that is the very essence of our being."[8] In his consciousness-awakening book *The Heart's Code*, Dr. Pearsall tells the moving story of his heart's gentle guidance that led to his miraculous healing from Stage IV lymphoma, a deadly form of cancer of the lymph system.

He tells equally touching stories of profound life-changing experiences of certain heart-transplant recipients, those whom Dr. Pearsall describes as "cardio sensitives."[9] These people recount that since their heart transplant they experience life differently, that their emotional reactions and in some cases their desires and patterns of behavior have changed. Family members verify that their loved ones have undergone major personality changes.

Amazingly, the "new personality" of the recipient is dramatically like that of the donor. The transplanted heart seems to be conducting its new orchestra of cells to "play" the song of the heart donor, thus changing the personality of the transplant patient.

In the same vein, heart transplant patients may voice information known only to the deceased donor. In one amazing case, an eight-year-old girl received the heart of a ten-year-old girl who had been murdered. When the child who had received the heart transplant began to have nightmares about being murdered, the concerned mother took her to a psychiatrist for help.

The little girl described the murder, including the murderer's clothing, weapon, time and place of the murder, so clearly that the therapist and the mother decided to notify the police. What the little transplant patient was remembering turned out to be completely accurate. In fact, the police tracked down and arrested the murderer through her description. He was later convicted. The chilling truth of this little child's "heart remembrance" was unqualifiedly verified.[10]

Dr. Pearsall concludes his inspiring book with his own heart's message: "If you close this book, sit back, become very quiet, ignore your brain's urging to get up and get going, and take plenty of time to sense the subtle code tapping in your heart and the other hearts around you, you will have the wondrous privilege of being a participant observer of the forging of your soul."[11]

Is it possible that our hearts' unique codes influence and direct the progress of our souls? We have learned that we may contact our Higher Self through meditating on the heart and that the heart is the seat of our higher intelligence. Through Pearsall's data and that of other eminent researchers, we may very well come to conclude that the heart, rather than the brain, is the physical center of our God-given higher intelligence.

Is the heart's code our Maker's way of interacting with our souls? It is fascinating that as science today is beginning to describe inner processes that mystics have understood intuitively, we increasingly approach the merging of scientific inquiry and mystical understanding.

Exercise for Attuning to Your Heart

1. *Offer a prayer to God, the angels and your loving Higher Self to help you attune to the vibrations of divine love in your heart.*

2. *Focus your attention on your physical heartbeat. It may help you to place your hand over your heart, just to the left of center of your chest, until you feel that gentle thump, thump, thump.*

3. *As you continue to pay attention to your heartbeat, pretend as if your breath were moving through the heart. Notice how the flow of the breath begins to synchronize with your heartbeat. Enjoy the relaxing feeling that comes with this practice as you stay with it for a moment or two.*

4. *Stay in touch with these pleasant sensations of breath and heartbeat while remembering a happy experience and an uplifting feeling that goes with it, such as love, compassion, joy, inspiration, gratitude, appreciation or "just plain fun."*

5. *Stay focused on your heartbeat, your breath and the positive feelings of your happy experience for two or three minutes.*

6. *Now ask your Higher Self for guidance. "What do I do now?" Or, "What is a good approach to this situation?"*

7. *Listen to the loving response of your Higher Self. It will be the very first awareness you have after asking the question. It may be words, an image or simply an inner knowing. It is often simple and brief.*

8. *Be aware that as you focus on your heartbeat, breathing and positive feelings, you offer your heart, brain and emotions the opportunity to move into "entrainment" or synchrony.*

9. *Take time to observe and enjoy the gentle synchronicity between your heart, brain and physical processes.*[12]

CHAPTER TWO

Exploring
the Sacred Miracle
of Adeptship

He who knows others is wise.
He who knows himself
is enlightened.

—LAO-TZU

*A*depts through the ages have demonstrated the power of divine love to heal and transform mind, body, soul and spirit. Saints and sages from time immemorial have mastered difficult times by asking Father-Mother God for help and being obedient to the inner quickening of guidance or direction. Through spiritual practices and a posture of nonattachment, they have gleaned an understanding of the higher purposes of life's cycles.

They have come to the enlightened realization that life is all about coming to know one's self, learning to love and help others and exercising will and determination to fulfill one's inner destiny. From this perspective, the need to compete with others, to vie for position or power or to focus solely on material gain vanishes.

As we progress on our journey of love and enlightenment, we, too, may choose to become adepts of compassion. We may offer to our loved ones, friends, neighbors and everyone we meet a cup of loving kindness that quenches the thirst of the soul. By so doing, we move ever closer to fulfilling our reason for being—to be vessels of divine love in a world that is hurting and in such need of love and comfort.

Yet, sometimes we disregard the loving inspiration and

gentle nudge from our Higher Self—especially when we feel burdened or overwhelmed with career pressures or difficult personal circumstances.

We may unconsciously try to protect ourselves from pain by toughening up and hardening our hearts. We may even close ourselves off from the help of friends as we paddle here and there trying to keep ourselves afloat in the sea of change.

This kind of drama may occur when we need to compete for an upgrade in a position or lose a job and have to apply for a new one. Or perhaps we face a family crisis or misunderstanding with friends or a difficult conflict in a relationship that is important to us. We might experience a sudden reversal in health or finances. These and a myriad of other scenarios may create that inner sense of scrambling to make it.

In the midst of such turmoil, instead of cheerfully greeting each happening in a mode of heart-centered entrainment, we typically succumb to an inner state of stress that signals "hyper-alert!" to all of our mental, emotional and physical processes.

Constant Hyper-Alert Thrusts Us Into a Survival Mode

What happens to us when we are on hyper-alert? We find ourselves thrust into the human survival mode: Fight, flight or freeze! Our body moves into high gear. Our mind races, the heart beats faster, the adrenaline pumps, and we feel a surging of energy.

We have entered the initial stage of stress, which Hans

Selye, the scientist who originally defined the stages of stress, called the "alarm reaction."[1]

During the inner ringing of the stress alarm, unless we freeze in place, we respond with what is aptly named the "fight or flight" mode of operation whereby our bodily defense systems quickly mobilize to handle the threat of danger. We feel fully alert and ready for action.

If the stressful situation continues, our physical body moves into a "stage of resistance" where fight or flight adaptation remains optimal in terms of bodily resources. We continue to be alert and to function efficiently.

However, when this state of hyper-alert continues over time and we keep trying to speed up our response to repeated crisis situations, a flood of information, complex job demands or problematic personal dilemmas, we begin to feel anxious, overwhelmed and exhausted.

What is happening here? As the ongoing barrage of input or demand for action has continued to mobilize the alarm reaction, we have begun to deplete our mental, physical and emotional resources. Our body is signaling us that we are paying a very high price for our continuing over-accelerated response mode.

If there is no relief, we eventually move into a "stage of exhaustion," where we are physically and psychologically depleted. In this stage we are vulnerable to emotional collapse and to physical problems such as hypertension, heart problems and immune system deficiencies.

Internal Reaction to Ongoing Mayhem Creates Battle Fatigue

In World War I and II, army doctors came up with the diagnosis of "battle fatigue" for soldiers going through the stress syndrome. If not countered, the internal process could ultimately be fatal, which is why the army had to figure out a way to deal with it. They began to rotate men out of the front lines to get some rest and regain equilibrium. Regular R & R (rest and relief) became a part of armed forces battle procedures.

Today it is well documented that war veterans and other people who have gone through extremely traumatic events, such as torture, rape, violence, accident, flood, fire or other catastrophes, may suffer from what is known as PTSD, posttraumatic stress disorder.[2] For these survivors, the traumatic event remains a dominating psychological experience that continues to evoke intense panic, anxiety, dread, grief or despair.

Individuals with PTSD may experience nightmares, daytime fantasies or actual flashbacks to the original trauma. As with any kind of pain, traumatic experience is filtered through our cognitive and emotional processes and influenced by previous events in our lives. Thus, although PTSD is no longer considered unusual, not all people who undergo extreme stress develop PTSD.

As we move along in the twenty-first century our battles are not limited to armies. Most of us are quite aware of the ongoing jockeying for power and position in society today and the resulting chaos and conflict in the political, cultural, scientific, corporate, religious and educational arenas of the world.

Like it or not, many of us are swept along by the outer turmoil as we inwardly try to keep pace as well as keep our balance. People from all walks of life tell me they need surcease from the outer frenzy and inner turbulence they are experiencing in major arenas of their lives. Their internal reaction to the ongoing mayhem creates today's version of battle fatigue in their bodies, emotions and mental processes.

Even if we are not directly involved in obvious chaos and conflict, we are often on the receiving end of information about it by way of the media or through friends or neighbors. Our internal alarm reaction is triggered, which in turn sets off the stress syndrome. We pay a physical and emotional price for absorbing jarring information—particularly when it arouses fear.

Fear is a powerful discordant frequency that moves us away from the higher vibrations of the heart. Psychologically, other discordant emotions such as anger, hatred, jealousy, depression, unhappiness or loneliness often have fear at their root.

Fear itself is very often the result of hurt. We receive information that scares us because of potential hurt to ourselves or loved ones, or it reminds us of hurts we have experienced in the past. We run scenarios about past or future hurts in the movie theatre of the mind. In such moments of apprehension, we are not centered in our hearts or focused on love, peace and gentle renewal. We are running scared inside.

Many people today experience fear and other intense emotional reactions from the stress of being tossed and turned by the turbulence of change. While some changes are situational or localized in jobs, relationships, homes, schools, churches and communities, others stem from the impact of national crises or international hot spots.

Planetary changes, such as shifting and disruptive weather patterns, major changes in the world's economies, threats of war, terrorist activities or major natural disasters often trigger the additional element of a sense of helplessness. We may be upset and worried about such happenings but usually feel we can do little or nothing about them. Whatever the source, the internal impact is much the same —*internal stress and survival mode functioning.*

Keeping Our Balance While Surfing Turbulent Waves of Change

Like it or not, most of us realize that handling the turbulence of change and the accompanying stress is an ongoing challenge today. Some people have learned to "surf" the waves of change expertly or at least with some equilibrium, while others look for quiet waters and find themselves at a loss when a safe harbor doesn't appear. Still others "play ostrich" and bury their heads in the sand, figuratively speaking, hoping the whole thing will just go away.

As the waves of change propel us toward new shores, we either become more and more adept at staying on our feet or we lose our balance, flounder, sink and lose confidence in ourselves.

I view the influx of change in the age of Aquarius as a physical and spiritual initiation, both individual and planetary in nature. Physically, as individuals, we are called to maintain a sense of inner peace and balance and at the same time accelerate our spiritual attunement to keep pace with planetary changes.

When we are stressed, fearful and shrinking from the challenges at hand, the electrical frequencies of our heart move into disorderly, chaotic patterns; our stress reaction has a field day. This is not good news. As we have discussed, emotions such as fear, anxiety, frustration, anger, hatred, irritation or annoyance interfere with our body's synchronous functioning and any sense of peace or flow of love and creativity we may have garnered.

How do we recognize the common symptoms of being stressed out? We may find ourselves uptight or getting overly irritable or emotionally reactive at home or on the job. We may experience insomnia, bad dreams or waking up frequently during the night. Or we might develop indigestion, headaches, muscle aches, ulcers, high blood pressure, heart palpitations or a depleted immune system. All of these are physical flags signaling us to reduce our level of stress.

These days most of us can't simply retreat into a cave or a mountain hermitage. Instead, people join health clubs, go on weekend healing retreats and try out spas, massage therapy and various exercise programs, all to get some relief from the bombardment of information and decision making and the stressful sense of being overwhelmed.

These methods help to some degree. But when we flip to the news on TV or check our E-mail, phone messages and schedule of meetings on Monday morning, the stressful reality of information pounding in hits us all over again. We need to find a new way to handle the bombardment of incoming information that assaults us daily.

A Shift in Perspective: Observing and Listening from the Heart

How about shifting our perspective? What if we decide to look at the flow of information as an opportunity for creative stimulation and choose to adopt an attitude of observing and listening from the heart for whatever sparks our own creative process?

Whenever we feel that inner stirring of interest or intuitive resonance, we can jot down some notes about our experience. We can become inventors, with ideas and tidbits of information as our raw material.

As we record the aspects that ignite our own creative spark, we can reconfigure the information to connect with our interests and just let the rest go by. We have extracted what is useful to our own creative process—and that is enough. Or we may choose to be simply an observer of the outer drama while we attune our "inner ear" to the prompting of our Higher Self.

The still, small voice of God often whispers the perfect solution when we open our hearts to discern positive vibration, higher motive, right thought and correct action from a point of centered awareness and nonattachment.

Spiritual teachers of the East and West have taught prayer, meditation and communion with Universal Love through the flow of the breath and the opening of the heart. They have taught us by word and example that love is the alchemical key to self-transcendence and oneness with Spirit.

What would happen if each one of us were to choose to offer love and compassion to others as Jesus did? Or to focus upon our God in a state of "listening grace" as did Mary, the mother of Jesus? Or to meditate on the wisdom of Confucius, enter the peace of the Buddha, extend to one another the mercy of Kuan Yin? Or to practice any of the virtues of the Great Teachers sent to remind us who we are as beloved sons and daughters of the Father-Mother God?

Think about it. Our lives would undoubtedly change for the better. If enough of us worldwide chose to do this, our world would become a better place to live.

Perhaps you do not consider yourself to be particularly religious. That's okay. It's more about spirituality than religion as a formal doctrine. It is a matter of developing an awareness of the positive intention and intuition of our heart and using only the information that really registers on us. It's like pitching the unopened junk mail into the trash and opening only what we really want to read.

When we observe, listen and respond from the heart, our soul, mind, emotions and body are at peace. In this state of inner synchrony, we are at our creative best. We are also in harmony with the vibration of the earth and earth changes, which is to our benefit physically, emotionally, mentally and spiritually.

Preparing for a Cosmic Process of Renewal and Transcendence

Geological records of the earth indicate that previous cultures have experienced cycles of major change similar to those occurring on the earth today. Ancient cultures have left evidence of transformational experiences during such periods of change through architectural ruins, myths, legends and sacred traditions passed along over the ages.

As Gregg Braden, geologist, author, lecturer and guide to sacred sites throughout the world, puts it: "We are living the completion of a cycle that began nearly 200,000 years ago, and a process of initiation that was demonstrated over 2,000 years ago.... In past ages, through proper initiation, these special conditions were utilized for clearer access to higher states. Now we don't have to recreate them in specialized temple chambers. We don't have to go anywhere. We are living in a global initiation chamber, with these geophysical conditions occurring on a worldwide scale. It's as if Earth herself is preparing us for the next stage of evolution."[3]

Braden's data indicates that the earth and everyone living on the earth are moving through a transitional period where the planetary magnetic field is diminishing and the basic vibrational frequency of the earth is increasing. Each one of us is affected by such changes in the earth's energy field because we are linked to the earth through our own electromagnetic field.

How does this work? Most of us are somewhat familiar with Einstein's theory of relativity, $E=mc^2$, meaning energy converts to matter and vice versa. It is in keeping with the conversion of energy to matter that as the magnetic field of earth diminishes and the vibrational frequency of the earth increases, the physical form of the earth is likely to change. *As citizens of planet Earth, we would also receive the impetus to change—vibrationally, magnetically, mentally, emotionally and physically.*

Braden's research suggests that every cell of our being, including our physical heart, is already striving to match the accelerating vibration of the base resonant frequency, or heartbeat, of planet Earth.

How does this process impact our physical bodies? We may think of ourselves as solid but in actuality our bodies are made up of energy in motion—traveling at various frequencies, yet densely packed enough to appear solid. Our memories, emotions, ideas and aspirations are also energy—traveling at still higher frequencies to appear relatively invisible but still quite tangible to our consciousness.

As our hearts, souls and bodies attune to the higher

vibrations of the planet, we are inwardly setting ourselves to adapt more successfully to the changing energy patterns of the earth. On a spiritual level, we seem to be synchronizing with a cosmic process of renewal and transcendence.[4]

Expansion of Consciousness for Soul-Renewal and Self-Transcendence

We know from the records of the ancients, mystics and scientists of today that our personal magnetic energy field goes well beyond the physical body to form what is called the aura. According to mystical teachings, the aura is a "field of energy surrounding the soul and the four lower bodies* on which the impressions, thoughts, feelings, words and actions of the individual are registered. It has been referred to as the L-field, which some scientists say controls the manifestation of the physical body."[5]

Many scientific fields work with these more subtle energies. For example, Chinese medicine works with the energies of the aura and the body through adjusting the movement of the life force, or ch'i, or prana, which is distributed along the meridians to every cell of the body.

This subtle energy may signal physical disturbance well before physical ailments appear. Practitioners of Chinese medicine use techniques such as acupuncture or acupressure to help clear the body of blockages to the movement of that life force, thereby assisting physical health and vitality.

We know from the work of Hans Jenny and his suc-

*Our physical, emotional, mental and etheric bodies. The etheric body contains the divine blueprint and all memories of the soul.

cessors that every sound projected into matter creates a pattern; when the vibration changes, so does the pattern; when the vibration stops, so does the pattern. Higher frequencies cause more complex images.[6]

Thus, sound projected into matter alters both the form and complexity of matter through the impact of specific vibrational frequencies. This goes along with a phenomenon most of us are aware of—a soprano shattering a glass by singing a prolonged high note.

Seasonal Affective Disorder, better known as the SAD syndrome, is another illustration of the impact of energy upon matter. In this case, people who are deprived of sunlight over lengthy periods of time develop symptoms of depression. Yet when the sun comes out or they are exposed to full-spectrum light, their symptoms tend to disappear.

Most of us know how much better we feel when the sun is shining—our bodies feel good and we have a sense of inner happiness. This is not entirely psychological. It is also a physical reaction to the influx of the higher frequency of light from the sun.

We may also remember how good it feels to stand before a magnificent waterfall or to walk beside the ocean when the waves are cresting and crashing against the shoreline. Again, that good feeling is not due simply to the beauty of these scenes. It is also the result of our absorbing the negative ions being released into the atmosphere through the rushing water.

Animals are also sensitive to energy changes in the

atmosphere and behave accordingly. They grow heavy coats in the winter and shed them as the weather warms up. Bears hibernate. Birds fly south for the winter. Animals and other wildlife seem to sense the vibration of changing weather before it is visible to the naked eye. I remember once seeing a whole herd of cattle lying down at an odd time of the day just before a big thunder and lightning storm.

In another arena of experience, Uri Geller bends steel through the power of his mind, advanced yogis defy gravitational force through levitation, and Indian fire-walkers make their way through hot coals without burning their feet. The visionary children of Medjugorje are impervious to pain while they are in an exalted state during their celestial visions of Mother Mary.

These various phenomena demonstrate the fact that matter and energy are interchangeable and that a change in our state of consciousness may actually alter our normal bodily reactions. They show that we can choose how to be affected by events that impinge on us. This is very important when we encounter worldwide changes.

Preparing Ourselves to Meet Planetary Changes

The drama of planetary transformation is coming ever closer to home by way of the impact on our physical bodies, our thoughts and feelings and our relatedness to one another.

How can we best prepare ourselves for these oncoming changes? Understanding is the first step. We can understand that our bodies are energy in motion that resonates with earth changes. What we perceive, envision, think and feel generates corresponding patterns within the liquid crystalline energy of our bodies that we call bone, muscle and tissue.[7]

Thus, we may prepare to meet earth changes by pursuing the mastery of our own personal energy fields. We may practice attuning ourselves to our higher heart frequencies[8] by meditating upon our God and remembering the sweetness of inspirational moments in our lives. We may choose to enjoy the beauty of nature, to surround ourselves with inspired forms of music, art and sculpture, to reach out to help others in need and to share with others our stories of joy, inspiration, appreciation and gratitude.

We may accelerate our higher consciousness by offering prayers, mantras and affirmations whereby we invoke the light of Spirit to infuse the soul, mind, heart and body with divine love. This practice goes back to ancient times when priests and priestesses practiced the creative power of sound to praise their Creator and to invoke divine blessings to heal and enlighten the people.[9]

As we synchronize our consciousness with the higher frequencies of our hearts, minds, emotions and physical bodies, we may keep pace with the acceleration of earth's vibrational frequency—and our soul's spiritual evolution.

We may see this process as a gradual speeding up of all levels of the physical vehicle of the soul, analogous to what we do when we travel in an airplane. The pilot gradually accelerates and the plane lifts into the air, climbing ever higher. As we gradually accelerate our vibration at the physical, emotional and mental levels, we rise spiritually, climbing ever higher. Mystics of all ages have understood this process as preparation for the alchemical wedding of soul and Spirit.

In past ages, this acceleration has been assisted by the special geometry of holy places. For example, both mystical tradition and scientific research indicate that the Great Pyramid in Egypt was an ancient temple where adepts trained for these initiations. The Great Pyramid stands as a monument to this advanced path of mastery that the adepts have walked before us.

Esoteric traditions teach that Jesus Christ, the Piscean Master, demonstrated adeptship in this initiatic process as he lived the alchemical transitions and initiations that we call the transfiguration, resurrection and ascension.[10] With each initiation his rate of vibration accelerated until even his physical body became totally one with Universal Light.

Yet we know that two thousand years ago Jesus lived in a human body even as we do today. He had to make choices in his life as we do. He dealt with human thoughts and emotions and the stresses of a physical body. And he did so with Christly aplomb as he demonstrated true inner strength and fortitude, inspired wisdom and understanding, and divine love and compassion.

Jesus taught by word and by example. He was a living, walking example of the love of God for His people. By example Jesus taught all of us many lessons: how to master our lower nature, how to overcome fear through courage and love, how to meet adversity with faith and charity, how to call forth the light for healing and blessing, how to take a firm stand for what we believe, how to be "wise as serpents and harmless as doves" in our everyday lives, and how to be true to ourselves and to our God in every action, word and deed.

Even as Jesus came to earth as the "light of the world,"[11] do you suppose we are meant to do the same? I believe we are. Let us follow his injunction not to hide our light under a bushel.[12] Every time we meditate, pray and invoke the light of God, we amplify the energy of divine love within ourselves and accelerate our vibrational frequency. We do the same when we follow the Golden Rule and behave lovingly and compassionately to others.

I believe that in these times of fast-moving cycles of change, we are called to become modern adepts of change by following the example of the Ancient Ones who have preceded us. Their stories of transformation and self-transcendence have been passed down through legend, folklore, sacred writings, fairy tales and the narrative tales of heroes and heroines—some of which you will read about in this book.

Exercise in Handling Personal and Planetary Change

1. *Begin each day by asking for specific guidance and listening intuitively to the responding counsel of God, your guardian angels or Higher Self.*

2. *Whenever something chaotic is happening, practice mentally stepping aside and observing the happenings around you from the perspective of an objective observer.*

3. *Make it a point to be fully aware of, but not to identify with, any turbulent or fearful emotions within you or in people around you.*

4. *Periodically throughout the day, take a moment to consciously relax and lovingly appreciate someone or something.*

5. *In the face of outer chaos, choose to center yourself, make a balanced decision and take loving, creative and constructive action in your own particular sphere of influence.*

CHAPTER THREE

Awakening the Gifts of Our Inner Hero

We take our shape, it is true, within and against that cage of reality bequeathed to us at our birth; and yet it is precisely through our dependence on this reality that we are most endlessly betrayed.

—JAMES BALDWIN

*E*ach of us has an inner hero who may be sleeping yet needs to awaken and come alive for our self-transformation. And for every heroic aspect of ourself there is a negative "shadow" side—archetypal base instincts that may undo the hero until he brings those hidden aspects into conscious awareness. Just as we are poised to claim our heroic nature, we may find ourselves caught in unconscious shadow patterns.[1]

How? We mean to be honest but find ourselves not telling the truth. We want to be courageous yet allow ourselves to be overcome with fear. We desire to love others and find ourselves dwelling on what we do not like about them. And the more we try to repress our negative feelings, the more they seem to rule us.

We can outwit our shadow side by exposing it to the light of self-awareness. What does that mean? It means to be fully aware that we don't want to tell the truth, that we are fearful, that we do not like something or someone. Once we are aware of our flaws, we can choose to tell the truth even if it brings repercussions, to claim our courage in the very face of fear, to behave lovingly to difficult people.

Redeeming Our *"Puppet-Like" Shadow Nature through Conscious Awareness*

Our shadow aspects may be redeemed when we bring them to conscious awareness. Their power is in their hidden nature. Once we choose to be fully aware and face the shadow head on, it no longer has power over us. And its negative aspects may be transformed.

If we remain unaware, we are likely to move through life repeating patterns established in our childhood, youth or even, perhaps, previous lifetimes. We can become so used to these patterns that we lose track of who we really are as men and women who have a unique identity, as souls who have come to earth for a special purpose. Instead, we identify with our habitual ways of thinking, our typical emotional reactions, our routine behaviors and ways of interacting with others.

When caught in our world of habit, we move through life as wooden puppets—one foot in front of the other, in lockstep with other people who are also entrapped in old mind-sets, automated feelings and engrained behavior patterns. We may not even realize that we are out of touch with our Higher Mind and true feelings, that we have closed down our heart, and our head is marching along on its own.

Some of us are like walking, talking encyclopedias of information, with schedules to keep, meetings to attend, reports to make—only dimly aware of the missing elements of open-heartedness, intuitive awareness, creative genius and inspired action. Others of us are puppets to the emotions—given a problematic situation we, as if on cue, can be counted on to flame into anger, burst into tears or retreat into tight-lipped silence.

Perhaps you aren't one of the marching band of puppets, or perhaps you are and have not realized it. Do you sometimes unthinkingly follow rules to the letter of the law at the expense of your own ethics or creative ideas? Or do you unthinkingly rebel against rules simply because you can't stand to be controlled? Do you stuff your real feelings at the slightest hint of uncomfortability? Or try to cover them up with a diversionary tactic, such as a show of power or outrage?

Do you find yourself trying to please at all costs whether at the office, with friends or family? Or do you pretend it doesn't matter when someone gives you that raised eyebrow look? Are you a more withdrawn person at work than you know yourself to be when you are on your own time? Does your streak of creativity seem to elude you when you need it most?

If you answered yes to any of these questions, you have found your inner puppet. Pulled by the strings of other people's rules, opinions, needs, and reactions, as well as by your own inner puppeteer, you become the conglomerate of habitual ways you think, feel and act in the presence of discomfiting circumstances. Locked into automatic reactivity, we often function more like a puppet than the person we really are.

The story of Pinocchio is very apt here. While the original nineteenth-century literary classic was the creation of Italian author Carlo Collodi,[2] most of us are more familiar with the twentieth-century Walt Disney adaptation, released as a movie and children's book. The drama of Pinocchio's transformation from a puppet into a "real boy" brings out heroic principles useful for us to understand as we seek to become our own real person.

The Story of Pinocchio as a Lesson in the Negative "Shadow"

As you may remember, the wood carver, Geppetto, gazes out his window at the starry heavens above and wishes upon a star that the puppet, Pinocchio, he has carved and painted might be a real boy. His words have been echoed by children ever since, "Star light, star bright, first star I see tonight, I wish I may, I wish I might, have the wish I wish tonight."[3]

I remember, as a child, eagerly watching for the first star in the night sky over Arizona and doing the very same thing. Have you? Have your wishes come true? Collodi must have known that angels listen and respond to the hopes and dreams of parents and children. And, of course, fairies are a classical way of describing angels, especially in children's stories.

Thus, the beautiful Blue Fairy answers Geppetto's wish and brings his puppet, Pinnochio, to life with a touch of her magic wand. However, he is not yet a real boy, for he has yet to face the challenge of his naïve instinctual character.

At the onset of the tale, Pinnochio pretty much represents a bundle of unconscious impulses, the good and the not-so-good—his shadow side, as Carl Jung described it.

We will see how Pinocchio's "shadow" sets the stage for his troubles and almost does him in. We will also come to understand his opportunity to redeem his negative shadow patterns when he chooses to follow his heart, listen to his conscience and take courageous, right action. We will look at our own process of shadow redemption as we learn from Pinocchio.

The Blue Fairy tells him that for Geppetto's wish to come totally true, Pinocchio must prove himself to be brave, truthful and unselfish. He must learn to choose correctly between right and wrong. She tells Pinocchio, "Be a good boy and always let your conscience be your guide."

We may ask ourselves, Do I honor my conscience, my inner sense of right and wrong, as my inner mentor, my daily guide?

Pinocchio is very happy that the Blue Fairy has brought him to life to be Geppetto's little puppet-boy. He really loves his father, Geppetto. He definitely wants to be a good boy. *But* he hasn't been tested yet. He has to learn a lot of lessons in the school of hard knocks before he earns his right to be a real boy.

As a curious and adventurous puppet-boy, he is often off track exploring in the wrong places or empty-mindedly having a good time with the wrong people. Also, naïve, instinctual puppet that he is, he lets nearly everyone pull his invisible strings.

We may ask, Has naïveté, curiosity or empty-mindedness ever led me into problematic situations? Have I mastered those shadow parts of myself?

As our story continues, quite forgetting the Blue Fairy's admonishments, when Pinocchio gets himself in trouble and gets caught, he tries to get out of it by telling a lie. Almost every time he faces temptation, he gives into it. And he is an absolute dope when someone offers him a chance for adventure. He doesn't think ahead because he is just a puppet, you know. As a puppet he can't be expected to know right from wrong—or can he?

For example, let's take one of Pinocchio's major faults, lying to keep from getting into trouble. The Blue Fairy has given him a very physical reminder when he doesn't choose to be truthful. Every time he tells a lie, his nose grows longer. As we shall see, his nose grows very, very long when he tells lie upon lie about his misadventures.

I wonder how each one of us might change if we were to discover that every time we told a lie, big or small, our nose grew longer—especially if we realize that when we are not honest with ourselves, we may not even know if we are being truthful to others.

Listening To Our Own Jiminy Cricket Conscience

Now the Blue Fairy knows that Pinocchio is going to need help to make right choices. That's why she dubs friendly Jiminy Cricket, Pinocchio's "Conscience," to help him along.

Of course, Jiminy has to earn his stripes, too. He is a bit scatterbrained and isn't always in the right place at the right time. However, he is good-hearted and usually catches up with Pinocchio in time to bail him out—if Pinocchio chooses to listen.

The biggest problem is that Pinocchio only listens to Jiminy when nothing exciting is going on or he's in very hot water. The promise of mischief or adventure pulls his invisible strings to the point that he nearly always "forgets" or ignores his father's or Jiminy's advice and ends up in a peck of trouble.

Ask yourself, Do I listen to my conscience when something fun and exciting that goes against my deeper values is pulling on me? What is my vulnerability?

Instead of going to school, Pinocchio ignores Jiminy Cricket's advice and goes off with "Honest John," the Fox, and his sidekick, the Cat. He buys the crafty fox's lie that there's "an easy road to success" and gets himself sold to Stromboli, the gypsy caravan man, as the star of the marionette show.

Since Pinocchio has such a propensity to tell whoppers himself, it's not too surprising that he can't tell a liar when he meets one. The Fox and the Cat are laughing all the way as Pinocchio heads down the road of fame and disaster.

Now ask, Do I recognize Fox and Cat as that crafty mind (mine or someone else's) that is out to get something for nothing? Do I ever get fooled?

Stromboli bills Pinocchio as "the puppet without

strings." He is a great success, to his much greater sorrow. For when Pinocchio belatedly decides it's time to go home and tell his father, Geppetto, the great news of his puppet stardom, Stromboli locks him in a cage, laughs at his pleas to let him go, and starts driving his caravan wagon to the next village.

Let's check it out. Have I ever let success go to my head, left behind responsibilities to family or friends and been locked into a situation I later regretted? Do I recognize this happening as a blessing in disguise—*if* I choose to learn the lessons of humility, responsibility and discernment?

Now Jiminy Cricket as Conscience has failed as well because he bought the lie of Pinocchio's "success." When good-hearted Jiminy decides to catch up with the wagon to tell Pinocchio goodbye and good luck, he finds him locked in the cage overcome with grief and shame. Try as he might, Jiminy can't get the cage open.

Since neither pleading puppet nor belated Conscience can get Pinocchio out of his self-created disaster, the Blue Fairy comes to the rescue. In this way, our guardian angels will always help us when we are truly penitent.

Of course, Pinocchio at once proceeds to spin a tall story about why he's in this predicament instead of being safely in school. As he goes on and on, his nose grows longer and longer!

When he begs for mercy, the Blue Fairy warns him that she can help him only this once. She also takes advantage of the moment to admonish him: "A lie keeps growing and growing until it's as plain as the nose on your face!" Finally, she kindly shrinks his nose, admonishes him to be a good boy and frees him from the cage. Pinocchio and Jiminy Cricket jump out of the wagon and head for home to Geppetto.

Let's ask ourselves, Has my quest for adventure or self-importance led to disaster because I acted on impulse and didn't listen to my inner conscience or the prompting of my guardian angel? Have I ever told a lie that came back to haunt me? What did I learn? How may I apply this lesson to my life today?

Pleasure Island: Where All Our Dreams Come True—or Do They?

Enter once again the Fox and the Cat with a new scheme. They have just met the coachman who collects "stupid, disobedient little boys" and takes them to Pleasure Island where all their dreams of rollicking fun and destructive naughtiness come true. The coachman shows the Fox and Cat a sack of gold coins and offers to pay them well for Pinocchio.

As Jiminy and Pinocchio are racing each other home to Geppetto, Honest John and Sidekick Cat intercept Pinocchio. They examine him with great concern and convincingly argue that because he looks so sickly he needs to go to Pleasure Island for a vacation—which, unfortunately, sounds pretty good to Pinocchio. Out the window goes his resolve to be a good, obedient boy to his father, Geppetto. Once again he falls for a lie and hops aboard the coach to Pleasure Island.

We might ask, How many times have I fallen for a promise of something for nothing, fun and games with no responsibility, or a need for a so-called "vacation" when it's actually avoiding some kind of responsibility?

On the coach Pinocchio meets a boy, Lampwick, who is full of strut and bravado. When they get to Pleasure Island, they go about having fun being bad. It's pretty easy to see that Pinocchio is being a puppet all the way. Even though he has no visible strings, you might say he follows whoever strings him along.

Ask yourself, Do I have an inner Lampwick? Does his strut and bravado express the real me? Does he give me a sense of true inner strength? If not, what do I want to do about it?

Once at Pleasure Island, Pinocchio and Lampwick cut a destructive swath of uproarious fun, gluttony and disaster and end up playing pool and smoking cigars. When Jiminy catches up with Pinocchio in the pool hall, he is totally disgusted with him. He gives him a cricket tongue-lashing, quits his job as Conscience and walks out on Pinocchio.

Have we ever behaved so badly that our conscience took a vacation? Did we get in so deep that we decided we might as well be "hung for a sheep as a lamb"? What is our lesson here?

Moments afterwards, Pinocchio, to his horror, sees Lampwick turning into a donkey, which is the fate of all bad boys who come to Pleasure Island. Pinocchio is further terrified as he himself begins to grow donkey ears and a tail. Quite appropriate since he has been behaving like a jackass!

Pinocchio escapes from Pleasure Island just in time with the help of faithful Jiminy Cricket who, seeing the fate of the other boys, has a change of heart and comes back to help him after all.

Have we ever played the "jackass" by an irresponsible pursuit of our desires? What did we learn? How are we applying that lesson in our life today?

The Search for Geppetto and Pinocchio's Redemption

When Pinocchio and Jiminy finally get back home, they discover that Geppetto is gone. Worried about his puppet son, Geppetto had set out to find him and ended up being swallowed by Monstro the whale.

We see how repentant Pinocchio is when he finally realizes how he has let everyone down and put his father in jeopardy. He is also sadly aware that all of these misadventures have been his own doing. He has donkey ears and a donkey tail to prove it.

We might say, "It's three strikes and you're out, Pinocchio!" Strike one: He didn't heed the instructions of the Blue Fairy. Strike two: He didn't follow the fatherly advice of good Geppetto. Strike three: He ignored the voice of Conscience, Jiminy Cricket. Now he's out of a home, a father, and his opportunity to become a real boy.

At this point, even though his life seems hopeless, Pinocchio has the opportunity to redeem himself—as we all do. Have we ever found ourselves in the depths of despair, done a complete turn-around, asked God and those we have hurt to forgive us, and determined to make up for our mistakes?

When we take an honest look at our intentions, thoughts, feelings and actions, we can act on the good and transform the rest. Of course, this requires owning up to our character flaws, our unthinking mistakes and our emotional misadventures. It also means making amends to people we have hurt or let down in some way.

Pinocchio does exactly that as he finally sees the error of his wayward ways. He immediately sets out to find Geppetto, and with the help of Jiminy Cricket (to whom he is listening these days), to try to rescue him. They search for Monstro, who is sleeping on the ocean floor. Pinocchio comes upon the huge whale as he is taking in fish and water—Pinocchio is swept in, too. To his joy and relief, he finds Geppetto with his cat Figaro and goldfish Cleo living in their boat in the whale's belly.

Pinocchio builds a big fire inside the whale to make him sneeze. The whale does just that, and the contents of his stomach, including Geppetto, Pinocchio, Figaro, Cleo and the boat roll out of Monstro's mouth. Maddened by the fire, the whale chases them and smashes their boat to pieces with his tail.

Pinocchio, hanging on to Geppetto and swimming as fast as he can, gets to the shore just in time to escape Monstro's full vengeance. Figaro and Cleo are also washed ashore, and Jiminy Cricket finally catches up with all of them, late as usual but faithful as always. Pinocchio is lying face down in a pool of water, water soaked and lifeless, having given his life to rescue his father.

Geppetto sadly takes his lifeless puppet home and lays him out on the bed. Exhausted and grieving, he falls asleep —not realizing that Pinocchio's redemptive process is finally coming to fruition.

Now that Pinocchio has shown the heart of a real boy by risking his life for his father, the Blue Fairy returns and touches him with her wand. Even as Geppetto mourns his loss, Pinocchio is transformed into a real, live, breathing boy. Jiminy Cricket receives a gold medal with *Official Conscience* engraved upon it. Both have learned their lessons and accomplished the seemingly impossible through strength of heart.

In the words of the song that completes the movie, "When your heart is in your dreams, no request is too extreme. When you wish upon a star, your dream comes true."[4]

Transforming Our Inner Pinocchio into a Hero

We transform our inner Pinocchio into a hero when we determine to have heart, to stop our "puppet-like" pretending to be someone we are not, to be very honest with ourselves and to be true to the inner prompting of our conscience and our guardian angel.

We may choose to ask ourselves daily, What right step do I need to take today so that I will feel good about it tomorrow? Step by step, as we recognize and regret our errors, ask and receive forgiveness and make recompense, our consciousness is redeemed. In the light of God's forgiveness, we are transformed.

Whatever the outer outcome, we are going to feel pretty good because we are leading from the heart and taking the "high road" in the situation. We are no longer allowing ourselves to be pulled by circumstances, other people or our own outworn habits. With each right decision and opening of our heart to love and truth, we become more one with our Higher Self.

Fairy tales of all kinds are really all about human nature. The redemptive process begins within ourselves when we recognize and choose to redeem the shadow side of each inner character. Talk about change! Internal change is perhaps the most challenging and rewarding of all. And transformation of our inner shadow characters allows us to meet external change from a point of peace and equanimity because we are no longer at odds with ourselves.

Instead of being swept away by the powerful currents of change, we steady ourselves and keep moving forward on our life's journey. And who knows? One day when we have returned to the heaven-world, we may look back on our adventures on earth and understand that we lived our own heroic story of becoming real—just like Pinocchio. For, as we have seen, our misadventures on planet Earth are not unlike Pinocchio's. Ultimately, we too can become our Real Self.

Exercise: Who Is Your Inner Pinocchio?

1. *What are your inner puppet-like flaws? Your knee-jerk reactions? Your engrained bad habits?*

2. *What are the heroic aspects of your Real Self that you would like to claim to replace those puppet-flaws?*

3. *What are the gifts of your Higher Feminine* your own guardian angel, or Blue Fairy?*

4. *How can you claim those gifts and offer them to others in your daily life?*

5. *What are the special qualities of your inner father, Geppetto?*

6. *How do you express those qualities with friends and family?*

7. *How will you train yourself to listen to your Higher Self, your own Jiminy Cricket conscience?*

*The Higher Feminine, when capped, represents the feminine side of our androgynous Higher Self.

CHAPTER FOUR

Shift of the Ages:
Light! the Alchemical Key

Hope, like the gleaming taper's light,
Adorns and cheers our way;
And still, as darker grows the night,
Emits a brighter ray.
—OLIVER GOLDSMITH

On an energetic level, change may be defined as the shifting of vibrational frequencies and magnetic energy fields. Many scientists and philosophers today believe that we are now living in a transition period, a special time of change that the ancients referred to as the "Shift of the Ages."[1]

This is portended to be a time of unparalleled change: change in customs and cultures, change in technological advances, possible worldwide economic disruption and major changes in weather patterns, including the shifting of the earth through earthquakes, volcanic action, tidal waves, floods and possibly even polar shifts.

We have experienced some of these changes in recent years, most recently with the extreme weather conditions and accompanying earth changes associated with El Niño and La Niña in 1998 and 1999.

The ancients believed that during the Shift of the Ages the human body would also need to shift in vibration in order to keep pace with earth changes. Adepts trained themselves in temples such as the Great Pyramid to survive the extreme kinds of conditions portended for earth at such a time.[2]

Is it possible that what many feel as a sense of inner urgency or a feeling of scrambling to keep up is the inner signaling of body and soul that it is time to accelerate our vibration?

Light Is the Alchemical Key To Self-Transformation

How do we accelerate our vibration? Adepts throughout the ages have understood light as the alchemical key.[3] When our bodies and our auras are filled with Universal Light, our vibrational frequencies accelerate naturally.

For example, evidence from a 1978 Los Alamos lab study of what is believed to be the authentic Shroud of Turin indicates that the fibers of the linen were scorched from within by a high rapid intense heat source of bio-chemical origin unknown to us at this time.[4] Thus, it seems entirely possible that Jesus, the Great Adept, resurrected after the crucifixion as the result of a tremendous action of light within his body, which accelerated until every cell of his being became one with that light.

Even as we may understand the miracle of Jesus' resurrection in terms of the acceleration of the flow of light within his being, we may see the acceleration of planetary vibrational frequencies in our time as another potential miracle in the making.

We might ask ourselves, How may we so accelerate our own frequencies that we fill ourselves with the Universal Light that regenerates our life force? By so doing, it is possible that we may pass through major earth changes unscathed and transformed.

We experience that light when we pray or meditate, attune to our Higher Self, listen to the wisdom of our heart and cultivate the science and practice of compassion toward all.

As we move through this transition period, we find science

coming to its pinnacle with advances in chaos theory, evolutionary biology, quantum mechanics and field theory and consequent changes in the way we view the earth and ourselves.

We discover from science that we may move through the Shift of the Ages more successfully by learning to track trends and patterns rather than focusing on single events, by attempting to understand processes instead of simply analyzing structures. As creative thinkers interconnecting with one another, we gain new bursts of understanding. We envision new vistas for the next generation as scientific discovery, cross-cultural exchange and educational methods become increasingly interwoven.

We may evolve more humanity-centered solutions to planetary conflict and national upheaval as "think tanks" take seriously the scientific evidence of the higher intelligence of the heart and balance the brainstorming of ideas with the inner wisdom of the heart.

As the worldwide web stimulates vital information exchange and an understanding and appreciation of cultural diversity, we may look forward to more friendly relationships with people all over the world.

When we appreciate the eternal power and magnificence of nature and honor the spark of the divine in one another, we draw ever closer in consciousness to our Maker.

I believe that we are in for an exciting time as we stretch our minds and hearts to understand and make creative use of the insights we may gain from all that is being discovered. Each of us, in our own way, is on an inner journey as we master ourselves in the whirl of seeming chaos and accelerated change. My vision is that our souls are engaged in an inner alchemy—the alchemical process of self-transformation.

Stability Comes from Our Inner Spiritual Lodestone

How may we facilitate this alchemical process? How do we handle the impact of changing circumstances, access our creativity as rapidly as we need it to meet the challenges coming upon us and stay stable in the process? How do we anticipate what's going to be happening tomorrow so that we can be there with creative solutions? How do we stay in contact with our loving inner self?

The answer is beyond our intellect, however bright we may consider ourselves to be. It takes our Higher Self, our Higher Mind, which is accessed through our heart's meditation upon the eternal truths.

Stability comes from an inner spiritual lodestone—our faith, vision, values and principles of living. When I think of people who have gone through great hardship, who have made it through extreme poverty or lack of schooling or imprisonment or being driven out of their country, I believe it is an inner flame, an inner connection with Spirit that brings people through hard times. And that takes different forms: vision, values, principles, spiritual tradition.

Remember that great movie and Broadway play *Fiddler on the Roof* and how "tradition" was all-important to the father? When he faced losing his daughter, he was deeply

troubled. He went back and forth between his inner principles and values—his allegiance to his God, his love for his
daughter—until he came to a decision.

Whether we agree with his decision or not, he made it
from his inner conviction and generated the strength to go
on. And his daughter had to do the same thing. They came
to different decisions, but each was strong within their own
heart and soul. Again, when the entire village had to leave
their roots and relocate, it was their internalization of tradition that gave the people the faith to keep going.

Author-psychiatrist Victor Frankl, in his moving book
Man's Search for Meaning[5] describes how he and others
made it through concentration camp experiences during
World War II by creating some kind of meaningful vision
beyond the horror of the present moment.

He tells how he would trudge along in the cold on a
concentration camp work detail, imagining being in a
warm auditorium giving a lecture about his experiences
once the war was over. He describes how some people
made it through by dedicating themselves to helping others
in worse shape than they were, and how people who lost
any sense of vision or hope would simply lie down and die.

What struck me the most from this heartrending
description of the brutality and futility of war and man's
inhumanity to man was the fact that this stalwart soul had
survived by creating a vision of a meaningful future that
carried him through the living hell of the concentration
camp. He followed it through after he was freed—his com-

pelling book is that vision in written form.

Such courage and creativity in the face of disaster, the worst possible kind of change, came from within him. Victor Frankl mobilized inner determination to survive harsh change and severe adversity through his faith in the potential meaning of life under any conditions. Such has been the path of sages and saints throughout the ages.

Become an Adept at Handling Change

As we journey through times of great challenge and change, I believe each of us is being given a cosmic opportunity to understand the deeper meaning of life and to forge a victory for our soul. We become more adept at handling change, more adept at letting go of the old and embracing the new. Through each adversity we progress in spiritual adeptship and self-transformation.

As waves of change come rolling in, we may choose to center in our hearts, to contact our inner source of spiritual strength, love and peace, to envision the presence of angels of light illumining us. When we are heart-centered, we meet whatever negative experiences we encounter with strength, calmness and peacefulness.

As spiritual masters and adepts throughout the ages have discovered and so beautifully taught, it is when we open our hearts and minds to Spirit that we experience the flow of divine love and gentle inner guidance that pilots us through difficult times and periods of transition.

We instinctively depict guardian angels as radiating

with light. Light is the essence of Spirit, the spark of the Infinite that lights the way to illumination, to inner strength, to divine love. It is through paying attention to that divine light sparkling within us that we set our sights on new horizons, find our way to new shores of self discovery and ultimately fulfill our soul's destiny.

Accessing Our Inner Potential and Expanding Our Consciousness

When we listen to our heart's wisdom we learn to welcome today as opportunity and to remember yesterday in terms of lessons learned. Instead of holding onto uncomfortable scenes of the past, we choose to remember what will help us in the present or future. Instead of shutting down our heart and feelings, we choose to stay open to our higher wisdom and compassion. All the moments that we open our hearts to one another in trying situations and all the days that we live in the fullness of lessons learned become a springboard to a more hopeful future.

When I think of my own lessons of yesterday, I value the moments of imagination and intuitive understanding, qualities that were nurtured during difficult times when I was a child. I treasure my experiences with God and nature, the world of books, the land of dreams and the fun of visualizing the dramas I listened to on the radio.

I don't ever want to misplace my imagination and intuitive approach to life by becoming overly immersed in mastering technology, acquiring information, watching TV or browsing the Internet. I make it a point to balance information and technology with nurturing my inner gifts through nature, imagery and writing.

This is a lesson from past experiences that I apply in my daily life. The same is true for spiritual practices. Meditation, prayer and invoking and envisioning God's light as blessing all life are a part of my day. As I listen to my heart's song, seek partnership with my Higher Self and the Christ Mind[6] and muster the courage to be the "real me," I come ever closer to my God.

I believe that conveying our inner vision and understanding to others is also important because it creates synergy with friends and loved ones. When we share or brainstorm together, we transcend what either one of us alone may think we know. We resolve conflicts with solutions that often surprise and please us.

Each of us has our own unique identity, the special gift of who we are, who our Maker created us to be, that we are meant to offer to life. We also have our own psychology based on the specific qualities of our soul as well as particular life experiences. When we listen to our heart and soul, we discover our unique gifts and talents and how we may apply them to fulfill our life's destiny.

None of us is an exact replica of another person except in the case of identical twins, or twin souls.[7] But even identical twins or twin souls may develop differently as they choose to accent different talents, exercise different dimensions of consciousness or pursue different endeavors in a particular lifetime.

As we interact with one another, we tap into unseen and unrealized potential. When we listen to the voice of each other's soul, we open our minds and hearts to new possibilities and set ourselves to learn and grow. We become more of who we really are—as visionaries, as strong, creative people who find it exciting to make good things happen. When this is our posture toward life, we begin to surf the waves of change with a spirit of exhilaration and increasing expertise.

Handling Inner Woundedness and Karmic Predicaments as Spiritual Initiations

How do we handle really hurtful people and circumstances? When we stay attuned to our Higher Self, we can mobilize the inner strength and creativity we need. We cease to resent hardship but rather allow it to teach us. We choose to greet the process as a spiritual initiation where we go through "the refiner's fire"[8] and come out the other side of that fire purged, raised up, transformed and ready to fulfill our mission.

We thereby ready ourselves to attain our spiritual victory—even as Jesus and Gautama and all the saints and sages over the ages readied themselves to attain their victory and immortality.

We choose to follow the plumb line of truth. We pray to our Creator to give us inner knowing. We practice being true to ourselves and to our God and becoming graciously adept at handling people and conditions that challenge and try us. We are practicing the art of adeptship every time we choose to remain centered in our heart and to respond to a challenging situation in a creative rather than reactive manner.

Even as we strive to do this we may find ourselves challenged by a sense of inner woundedness from hurtful experiences and compensatory negative patterns we have adopted to protect ourselves from further hurt. At the same time, our soul understands that many of these happenings have been karmic in nature and that our soul matures in our expression of divine love when we forgive those who have wounded us.

What is karma? Spiritually, it is known as the universal law of cause and effect. For every cause we put in motion, there is an impact on life that comes full circle back to us. As the old saying goes, "What goes around, comes around" —a kind of cosmic boomerang.

In other words, what we dish out to life returns to us, offering a lesson in energy flow. We all enjoy the return of good karma, the positive energy and circumstances we have earned by being kind, helpful and loving to life. When this karma comes back to us, we experience inner growth and happy times in our lives.

We find it more difficult to "enjoy" the return of our not-so-good karma, where we are on the receiving end of hurtful energy we have sent out through being unkind, unhelpful and unloving to others in this or past lives. Yet our soul may have a certain sense of relief from realizing that this is an opportunity to balance karma and to learn a self-transforming lesson.

In truth, the return of negative karma often produces the most accelerated growth and self-transformation. Karma, good or bad, can be a great teacher to the soul.

How do we set ourselves to learn the lesson when we face a karmic situation? When difficult karma descends, we can choose to take a time-out, ask the angels to help us center in our heart and listen to the counsel of our Higher Self. As we do this, we enter a space of inner stillness where we experience a sense of clarity and an understanding of the karma and the karmic lesson.

With further meditation and contemplation, we come to understand how to respond in a positive way—thus coming full circle by balancing the karma of the past and creating a new round of good karma for the future.

Achieving Peaceful Nonattachment as the Buddha under the Bodhi Tree[9]

One way to learn a positive approach in a difficult karmic situation is to practice being the *divine observer* of our experience, even during hurtful moments. Meditation is a way of practicing nonattachment and self-observation, which is not a form of denial or shutting down of the emotions but a surrender and trusting in the universe as God. When we choose to take the stance of nonattachment and self-observation at the same time that we are thinking, feeling and sensing on a physical level, we move into a space where we are no longer entrapped by the experience.

I call this being "the Buddha under the Bodhi Tree" because Gautama Buddha attained his state of enlightenment through this very practice. As a Buddha-to-be, Gautama sat under the Bodhi Tree in meditative contemplation. He so centered himself in the bliss of nirvana that he was not reactive to Mara's[10] threats, attacks and tricks. He observed, felt and experienced all that Mara was doing as he remained in a state of peaceful nonattachment to the outer experience.

How did he achieve such a quiescent state in the midst of Mara's assaults? Gautama chose to remain in deep meditation upon his God even as his physical, emotional and mental being went through extreme testing. The fruit of this testing was his glorious state of enlightenment through which he brought forth the Four Noble Truths and the Eightfold Path.[11] These he would offer to all people for their surcease from suffering.

The last insult that Mara gave to Gautama was meant to be the final discouraging put-down, "It won't matter a bit if you are enlightened because nobody is going to listen to you anyway." Gautama Buddha simply extended his hand, touched the earth and said, *"Some* will listen." A very short and powerful response!

We need to remind ourselves that *some* will understand when we choose to be true to ourselves and to our God. *Some* will appreciate the gift of our heart's wisdom in difficult times.

When we look at trying circumstances from the Buddha's point of view of non-attachment, we realize that they are usually a full-circle return of energy patterns that we have sent out—sometime, somewhere. When we greet returning karma with a positive attitude and a determination to increase in self-mastery, the karma itself becomes a cosmic thrust that propels us into higher consciousness.

Thus, we may accept our karma as an opportunity for acceleration—spiritually, mentally, emotionally and physically. Or not. The choice is ours.

Buddha Under
the Bodhi Tree Exercise

1. *Invoke the presence of the Buddha to be with you as you sit under your own Bodhi Tree of higher consciousness.*

2. *In the presence of a difficult situation or inner burden, choose to focus your complete attention upon your heart and the movement of your breath.*

3. *Simply observe the situation or burden while staying in touch with the beating of your heart and the rhythmic flow of your breath.*

4. *Allow yourself to experience your specific thoughts, feelings and body reactions even as you maintain the posture of the divine observer who is surrendered to the universe as God.*

5. *Be aware of changes in perspective as you continue to be the nonattached observer of your experience.*

6. *Notice what you are learning as you experience the ebb and flow of the inner and outer drama from a point of nonattachment.*

7. *Repeat the Buddha under the Bodhi Tree exercise whenever you face a challenging circumstance in your life.*

CHAPTER FIVE

Chaos as Prelude to Personal Metamorphosis

*This world, after all our science
and sciences, is still a miracle;
wonderful, inscrutable, magical
and more, to whosoever
will think of it.*
—THOMAS CARLYLE

*T*he new science of chaos teaches that chaos is actually a creative force for change and a prelude to metamorphosis. It is an essential process through which Mother Nature organizes, renews and revitalizes her kingdom. A fascinating aspect of this process of change is that it is generated from within each natural system and is wholly self-organized. A chaotic nebula of gases coalesces into a spiral form and finally into planets with coherent orbits and relationships. A flower, a plant, or a tree comes into being from the interaction of random atoms and molecules with the order-creating instructions of DNA within the seed. And so do we.

In the great miracle of human life, randomness and determinism interact at every stage of the process of sperm production, ovulation and conception, so that a fertilized egg can begin its journey of life in the womb of the mother. Moving with invisible timing through an intricate process of cell division and stages of embryonic development, a new life begins. A soul enters the earth, clothed in flesh through the indwelling power of the Infinite in man and woman.

So what then is chaos? I believe chaos is the revitalizing, creative movement and flow of the Infinite One in all creation. To me the evidence is preeminent in the magnificent, ever-changing patterns in the heavens and the earth and in the complex interplay of opposing forces in the evolution of the consciousness of mankind.

Chaos is perhaps not really chaos at all, but rather an embryonic form of transforming change, the means by which we continually evolve in consciousness and increasing awareness of infinite possibilities.

Chaos theory is all about the remarkable ongoing process of creation that occurs moment by moment as energy and matter, thoughts and feelings, particles and magnetic fields collide, interact, and crystallize into new concepts and shapes. The chaotic movements of any system or interaction gradually self-organize to form a unique pattern not previously visible or even predictable, a type of boundary where order emerges out of chaos. This pattern, shape or boundary is known in chaos theory as a "strange attractor," the order inherent in chaos.[1]

As we study the process of chaos, we expand the narrow room of our human consciousness. We grow in awareness and appreciation of the Creator and Regenerator of all life. As we more and more comprehend the vastness and intricacies of the universe and our own planet Earth, we experience an increasing reverence and humbleness before our God.

We could view change as the interaction of the three figures of the Hindu Trinity: Shiva who destroys unreality, creating chaos; Brahma who creates new patterns out of the old elements and Vishnu who preserves and locks in the new patterns. An astronomer, speaking on the evolution of life in the universe, recently described this process as the interaction of chance, necessity and opportunity.[2] For example, there is chance, or chaos, in the outward movement of the "big bang" at the beginning of the universe (Shiva). There is also an interaction with laws of physics, such as gravity and inertia, which can be thought of as necessity (Brahma). The total available mass in the universe, which sustains this interaction, provides the opportunity (Vishnu).

It is interesting to note that this trinity of forces can also be expressed in Christian terms as Holy Spirit (Shiva), Father (Brahma) and Son (Vishnu). The interaction of these forces also occurs in the organic world. The evolution of life can be expressed as the interaction of random variation (chance) and selective reproduction (necessity) within the medium of the gene pool (opportunity). All growth, all creation, can be seen as the interaction of these three.

Thus we discover that, by taking a page from Mother Nature's handbook, we may learn to greet the chaotic nature of change as an opportunity for self-metamorphosis and transcendence. How does it work? Let's take a closer look at the science of chaos.

Chaos Creates Transformation and Renewal

Scientists have discovered that the moving and colliding of energy and matter, seemingly chaotic, create transformation and renewal. A simple example is the fact that although we cannot precisely predict our weather from moment to moment, weather patterns over time conform to certain boundaries, to an emergent order recognized only in retrospect.

The new sciences of quantum physics, chaos theory and biology are doing innovative research with chaos. One dramatic experiment was conducted from the space shuttle Atlantis. Scientists hypothesized that the aurora borealis (the northern lights) is an electrical-magnetic phenomena created by sun-charged particles called solar winds streaming toward the earth at supersonic speeds and intersecting earth's invisible magnetic field.

They tested their hypothesis by bombarding the earth's magnetic field with electrons fired from the space shuttle Atlantis. Sure enough, a glorious, resplendently colored, artificially created aurora borealis appeared in the sky from the waves created through the collision and interaction of the electrons and the magnetic field.[3]

Chaos theory suggests that information is the primary force in the universe, the source of all change. From a spiritual perspective, I believe that information is what makes up the many facets of the Mind of God, that God is the center of all information and that through creative use of information we are actually expressing a divine matrix.

Thus, the Universal Mind provides the divine raw material. It is up to us to use it wisely and compassionately to offer solace, comfort and inspiration to others, to come up with creative solutions to problematic situations and to expand the narrow room of our human consciousness.

When we access the cosmic information system, creative new ideas spring forth in our minds and hearts. In the very presence of seemingly chaotic interaction we find our vision expanding, our ideas multiplying and our consciousness opening to new and diverse ways of meeting the challenges at hand.

Scientist and business consultant Dr. Margaret Wheatley offers her understanding and development of chaos theory to help people relate to one another more constructively in today's complex business world. She believes that we have the opportunity to experience renewal and revitalization during chaotic times and that we can benefit from today's fast-moving cycles of change rather than sinking into despondency and non-productivity.

If we let go of rigid thinking and choose to interact, brainstorm and share with one another, we encourage what Wheatley calls "the participatory nature of reality" and its accompanying process of chaos to reconfigure our thinking. Through exchanging information we allow our inherent personal and organizational self-renewing properties to generate creative ideas and new approaches to the changing scene, whatever it may be.[4]

When we think about it, we realize that nature abounds with creative self-organizing systems that at times seem chaotic and destructive but are in reality life giving. Volcanoes erupt and create new landmasses; oceans beat upon rocks and beaches, wearing them down, changing the form of the earth.

Clouds move, seemingly chaotically, changing form, streaming out, bunching up, layering and whirling, holding water and releasing the moisture in rain or snow. Nature's own sprinkler system nurtures the earth, the streams, trees and vegetation, which in turn become life giving as they provide water, food and shelter for animals and people.

Sunshine in the mist following the storm forms a

shining rainbow of promise. Nature changes her garments with the seasons. We delight in the many shades of greenery and multicolored flowers of spring, in the bright, rich colors flashing in the summer, the golden yellows, flaming oranges, and deep burnt reds of autumn and the shimmering white of lacy snowflakes, icy ponds, frozen rivers and snow-packed mountains in winter. And then Nature goes to sleep for the winter as she completes her yearly cycle. The earth rests along with the hibernating bears—in preparation for a brand new cycle the following spring.

As spring returns, trees begin to leaf, flowers bloom and birds return from the south where they have spent the winter. Bears come out of hibernation, baby deer toddle after their mothers and butterflies emerge from caterpillars. Children romp and play in the sunshine, people plant their gardens and dormant tulip bulbs begin to bloom. Another round of life has begun.

How do these rounds of nature's yearly life cycle apply to each one of us in our longer life cycle of three score and ten—and beyond? The writer of Ecclesiastes says, "To every thing there is a season, and a time to every purpose under the heaven. A time to be born, and a time to die; a time to plant, and a time to pluck up that which is planted."[5]

When we take this teaching to heart, we put our roots down wherever we are, but we also prepare for transplanting as necessary. As has been said, "Home is where the heart is." We can be at home wherever we are when we open our heart and soul to life's cycles and lessons. We may welcome each seemingly chaotic interval as a new beginning, a new leg of the journey.

Transplanting Ourselves Can Be a Chaotic Process of Renewal

In our rapidly changing world, many people are changing jobs, relocating, moving their families, starting over again. Moving with the winds of change, transplanting ourselves, can be a chaotic process—but it is also potentially one of growth and renewal.

As one of my clients, Dave,* asked me some months ago, "How can I best prepare my family to be uprooted and moved to a new place? And how do I maintain an upbeat stance through this major job change when I realize I'm going to have to acquire new skills, maybe ultimately even a new career?"

This young man was asking reasonable questions out of loving concern for his family's welfare and a strong desire to stay positive through a major change cycle.

I reflected for a moment. "It's a lot to handle all at once, isn't it? Radical change is difficult. But I believe you *can* make the new job and move a positive experience for yourself and the family. First of all, you'll want to finish up your current job in a way that you will feel good about yourself. That's one priority. Right?"

Dave nodded, "Yes. When I look back, I want to know I gave it my best shot. But I have to start thinking about

---

*Names, places and some details have been changed to protect the anonymity of individuals in the case histories presented in this book.

the new job, too, or I won't be ready for it. Then there's the move. It's a lot to handle."

Many of my clients had gone through this process, so I had the picture. "It's called, overwhelm! Right?"

Dave smiled, "Yeah."

I decided to offer a few suggestions: "It helps a lot to focus yourself on one thing at a time. First, I imagine you need to give full attention on your workdays to winding up the job you have now. That will earn you a good reference. Second, how about taking time this weekend to write down specifically the steps you need to take to get ready for the new job? Once it's on paper, it's somehow less formidable. What do you think?"

Dave looked thoughtful. "That makes sense. It's been pretty chaotic trying to finish up the job I have now, so I haven't done much to prepare for the new one. And I do need to start transferring the details of my current job to whoever is going to take it over. If the higher-ups don't make a decision on that pretty quick, I'll just put it on paper for the next guy."

"That seems like a smart move to me," I responded. "What's next?"

Dave sighed, "Apart from the work thing, my wife and kids are uneasy about moving to a new city."

I could understood that one. "Sure they are. You probably are, too. Uneasiness in the face of change is perfectly normal. But once you start readying yourself and the family for the move, I can almost guarantee that everyone will begin to feel better."

Somewhat reassured, Dave brought up his next concern. "I know that's true. But another factor is that we've lived here for fifteen years and it's the only home our children know. It's hard to think about leaving here, even though I know we have to do it."

I gave him my perspective: "It's definitely challenging to uproot yourselves when you've been in one place for many years. It brings up feelings that each of you need to honor and share; when you share feelings as a family, everyone feels safe and supported. My own take on the process of uprooting and transplanting is that we need to do what we would do with our plants—keep ourselves warm, watered and fed in the process of transplanting, and prepare the earth in the new garden.

"I also see this as a metaphor for deeper questions. I know that you are serious about your spiritual path. What would your path suggest you do to keep the family spiritually and emotionally warm, watered and fed?"

Dave began to relax a bit. "I guess it would be praying for guidance. When Christine and I focus our prayers on a particular issue, we do get direction. I'd say that our souls feel warm, watered and fed when we do our spiritual work and all of us keep on loving each other."

I could feel the depth of Dave's love for God and his family. "That's a truly heartwarming way to look at it. I'm sure the inner guidance you are seeking will be there for you as you do your spiritual work. And loving each other through difficult times is what family is all about, isn't it?"

Dave was quick to answer, "Yes, we're pretty good at showing how much we love each other. The children have helped us learn to do that. They're so quick to give us a hug and ask for one, too. I can see that's the real foundation—prayers and loving each other.

"Since we're on the subject of feelings, do you have any special suggestions as to how I can help the family deal with their feelings? Christine is kind of uptight about the whole thing, and the kids are a divided house. Danny is jumping up and down with excitement, but Susie and Christy keep saying they don't want to move. I know they're scared."

I nodded. "It's normal that Christine would be a bit uptight and the girls scared. Probably Danny is too, but he's handling his feelings by jumping into his excitement. Take a hint from him. Share his enthusiasm, and lend a listening ear to Christine and the girls. You know how it is with us women. We handle our feelings by talking about them."

Dave smiled. "Yes, I know. I don't think I've felt much like listening because I've been apprehensive myself. But I realize they need to talk it out. It'll help me, too. And when I listen to Danny, I do feel my excitement coming to the surface. Maybe that's what I need to do—just let it come up instead of being 'Mr. Solemn and Determined.'"

Dave and I both laughed. "I think that's a great idea! The entire situation is going to seem less scary to the family once you settle the details of home and school in whatever city you are moving to."

Dave nodded. "We're moving to Denver. I have some vacation coming and we're planning to scout out the territory, visit some schools and pick out a neighborhood. I know we'll all feel better once we know where we're going to live and where the kids will go to school."

He had the physical details of the move under control. The issue was mostly everybody's feelings. So I said, "Yes, you'll all probably feel a lot more at peace once the details of home and school are settled."

Dave responded, "I know I'll feel more comfortable and at peace once I know where we are going to put our roots down. And that brings up another issue. We have to put our house on the market so that hopefully it can be sold by the time we leave. I know the family is dreading that part of it."

I reassured him, "I think the family will take selling the house in stride once they help find a new one. It's really fear of the unknown that makes a move seem so difficult. Once you jump in and start dealing with the unknown, it becomes a known quantity. As you deal with the specifics, everything kind of smoothes out."

Dave looked relieved. "I can see that. I feel better after having talked it over. I'll follow through and keep in touch, but I definitely have a clearer idea of how to help the family through the feeling stuff. We just need to talk about our feelings and start making specific plans."

We were winding down now, so I summed up my thoughts, "I believe you are totally on the right track, Dave, and I know how much it helps to talk it through with someone else. It's like new energy comes in and propels you forward. I think the major point here is to keep expanding your vision and exploring the new opportunity rather than holding on in any way to the cycle that is ending for you."

Dave looked like he was having a sudden "ah-ha." "Hey, maybe it's the 'holding-on' part that has been giving me trouble. I have to admit this whole thing is uncomfortable for me, too. I've been just as attached to my job and our lifestyle here as the family is.

"On the one hand, I know there is no point in holding on to something that's over. On the other hand, it's been hard to get a firm grip on the future because we've all been shaky about the change. I guess I'd better get to work on this 'letting-go' process you're always talking about."

We laughed together. He was right. I have a slight attachment to the letting-go process because I have found that most of our pain comes from holding on to something—a job, a way of life, old habits, a worn-out point of view, whatever we're leaving behind. Dave left the session with a battle plan and renewed determination.

He came in a few more times, and his wife came with him once. They had made a lot of progress. Dave had pretty well finished his present job to his satisfaction and was seeing the new job and the move as an excellent opportunity. Christine was planning her new home even as she was showing the old one to prospective buyers.

They took the trip to Denver as a family and were pleased to find schools and a neighborhood they liked and could afford. They put a down payment on a house in the suburbs and were looking forward to the sale of their present home. The last I heard the girls were getting more positive toward the move and Danny was still jumping up and down with excitement.

Claiming Inner Metamorphosis in the Midst of Tumultuous Happenings

Change *can* be positive. When we look to the horizon, bounce ideas off of our friends and family and stay open to our feelings as we move ahead with our plans, we create a new vision of our future. We experience an energizing sense of self-transcendence and find ourselves looking forward with hope to the future that we are in the process of creating.

It is this positive state of consciousness along with our expanded vision that draws new opportunities to us. And our internal transformation helps us to discover and enter into the necessary avenues to establish new skills, new relationships and new patterns of living.

When we allow chaos and the Mind of God to reconfigure our thinking, our vision and our perspective, we may claim our own creative process and inner metamorphosis in the very midst of tumultuous happenings. We become like the traditional picture of Kuan Yin, standing serenely on the back of a moving dragon,[6] surfing the waves of chaotic happenings with equanimity and greeting chaos as an opportunity for personal growth and regeneration.

Exercise: Using Knowledge of Chaos as a Compass

1. *Project yourself back to a time of chaos in your life. Where were you? With whom? Doing what? What happened? How did you feel? What did you learn?*

2. *How has that chaotic time in your past set a tone or pattern for you today? What have you learned from the process of chaos that you may apply creatively to your life today?*

3. *What chaos are you experiencing in the present? What do you desire to accomplish tomorrow? How may what you think, feel and do in response to the chaos of today set a positive tone for your tomorrow?*

4. *What chaos do you anticipate coming in the future? What have you learned from chaotic times of the past and present that you may use as a compass to guide you in the future?*

CHAPTER SIX

The Odyssey
of Self-Transformation

But O the ship, the immortal ship!
O ship aboard the ship!
Ship of the body, ship of the soul,
voyaging, voyaging, voyaging.
—WALT WHITMAN

*H*omer's Greek tale *The Odyssey* may be seen as a timeless story of the soul's striving for adeptship and the hurdles of initiation to be cleared in pursuit of true Selfhood. The drama that Odysseus* goes through may be viewed as a mythical voyage and as an inner odyssey of self-transformation and transcendence.[1]

Since Homer's epic drama is primarily the story of Odysseus claiming his true manhood, we will view it as a story about the masculine side of human nature. Women may not completely identify with Odysseus, but as we review his adventurous voyage we will notice how his initiations correspond to a woman's inner journey and the psychological patterns of her masculine side.

Simply put, the masculine side is that part of each of us, male or female, that is oriented to physical strength, inner empowerment, intellectual expertise and "doing." Our feminine, on the other hand, is the side of each of us that is intuitive, emotional, nurturing and relationship oriented. Whether man or woman, we pass through similar rites of passage as we seek to transform the unredeemed masculine or feminine parts of ourselves.

Odysseus is very like each of us in that he has both strengths and weaknesses. He is courageous, good hearted and enduring, a man of sharp wit and fiery determination.

*Ulysses, in Latin

He also has an impulsive nature, a temper and an arrogant way about him. Perhaps his greatest weakness is his incessant curiosity that leads him into all kinds of trouble that he could have bypassed had he let well enough alone.

He forges his way through a series of adventures that we may look at as representing his spiritual rites of passage. Odysseus is transformed from a foolhardy, stormy warrior to a seasoned and discerning adept who understands and claims the essence of manhood. With this transformation, he is ready for reunion with faithful Penelope who personifies his higher feminine nature and also represents his beloved twin soul or soul mate.

Psychologically, we may compare Odysseus' journey to our own as we also seek to forge our way through inner battles and temptations. We, too, need to learn our soul lessons and win the victory over our "dark side." How? By becoming fully aware of our human weaknesses and transforming them into the strengths of a true "king," which, esoterically interpreted, means the *key to the incarnation of God*.*

Lessons on the Homeward Voyage: The Price of Disobedience

Let us look at the homeward voyage of Odysseus, king of Ithaca and hero of the Trojan War. After ten long years of battle, his ingenious ruse of the Trojan Horse has finally ended the war. Helen of Troy has been safely returned to her husband, King Menelaos. It is time for Odysseus and his Achaian comrades to return home.

---

*This concept has been taught by Mark and Elizabeth Prophet.

Thus, they set out on a fateful homeward voyage, Odysseus eagerly anticipating his reunion with his wife, Penelope, and his young son, Telemachos. Yet, he has lessons to learn before the gods will allow him to return home.

What are the lessons? Odysseus must overcome pride and arrogance, learn to be obedient to the gods and to take right action under difficult circumstances. Being obedient doesn't come too easily to Odysseus because he is a king and has a big enough ego to think he always knows best.

His saving graces are a good heart and his reverence and trust for his spiritual mentor, Athena, daughter of Zeus, known as the "Goddess of Truth." We may see Athena as representing the "Higher Feminine." She depicts the divine level of the inner feminine we have already described as the intuitive, emotional, nurturing and relationship-oriented side of one's self.

Odysseus' men are a reflection of his own arrogance and start out by disobeying his orders. Seventy-two of them lose their lives at their first landing at Ismaros of the Ciconians. After killing the Ciconian men and plundering the city, the men revel and feast instead of obeying orders to return to their ships. They are killed by the surviving Ciconians before they can set sail.

What was Odysseus' and the men's lesson? They could have been benevolent to life rather than plundering and killing. We might say that the Ciconians returned to them "an eye for an eye, a tooth for a tooth."[2]

Was it worth the plunder and greed? What happened

to the true strength they might have gained from benevolence and forbearance?

We ask ourselves, Do I celebrate success in noble, uplifting ways? Or do I sink into greed and revelry? What other lessons may I glean from this experience of Odysseus and his men?

Land of the Lotus-eaters: "Sweet" Lure of Fantasy and Dreaminess

Odysseus and his remaining fleet sail on to the Land of the Lotus-eaters. The three men sent ahead to explore discover friendly people who offer them lotus, a honey-sweet fruit somewhat like a berry or poppy pod. As soon as they taste it they go into a dream world and forget all about returning to Ithaca. Odysseus has to drag the men back to their ships, tie them down and order the rest of the crew not to eat the lotus fruit.

We ask ourselves, Have I ever gone overboard on drugs, alcohol, nicotine, sex, gambling, television, food or anything else to the point that it took over my life? Is there any sweet lure of fantasy that stands in the way of accomplishing my goals in life? What is my lesson?

Encountering the Cyclops: The Fateful Outcome of Curiosity, Greed, Arrogance and Anger

Odysseus' next encounter is with the Cyclops, a race of one-eyed giants who live in mountain caves. Here Odysseus' curiosity and greed get the better of him. He goes exploring with his personal ship and crew and comes upon the cave of Polyphemus, one of the Cyclops giants.

Odysseus' men try to get him to take some of the Cyclops' goats and cheeses and leave, but he wants to stay and get more treasures from the giant. The Cyclops devours two of his men and blocks the cave so the rest are trapped.

The next day the Cyclops devours two more of the men. Then Odysseus offers the Cyclops wine to get him drunk. He tells the giant, "Noman is my name,"[3] after which the Cyclops drinks himself into a stupor.

Odysseus and his men heat a sharpened spike and drive it into the sleeping Cyclops' eye. He bellows with rage. He is blind and furious at being tricked. When the other giants ask who did it, the Cyclops says, "Noman did it." They tell him that if "no man" did it, the gods must have done it, and he will have to pray to his father, Poseidon, for help.

Odysseus contrives a way to escape from the cave by tying each man underneath three of the Cyclops' sheep when they go out in the morning. He himself hangs upside down under the biggest ram. The blinded Cyclops does not detect them even though he passes his hand over the backs of his sheep.

Once outside, the men dash to the ship, but Odysseus can't resist yelling an arrogant, mocking insult at the Cyclops. The angry Cyclops heaves a huge rock at their ship, creating a tremendous wave that washes them back to shore. His men beg Odysseus to lay off, but Odysseus, full of anger and pride, yells again to the Cyclops that he, Odysseus, is the one who has blinded him and, if he could, he would hurl him straight into hell.

Now the Cyclops knows who has blinded and outwitted him. He prays to his father, Poseidon, for a curse to be placed upon Odysseus. He asks that Odysseus never see his home again, or if he does, that he lose his companions and experience many miserable years before returning home to trouble and tribulation.

Odysseus has met the great magnifying mirror of his own arrogance and anger in the form of the Cyclops. As a result of his outrageous cockiness, he incurs the wrath of Poseidon that plagues him for years to come.

We ask ourselves, Do I have too much curiosity, a hint of greed, arrogance or anger or a tendency to make headstrong decisions? How may I transform those negative shadow qualities? What might I put in their place, e.g., acceptance and appreciation of what I already have? Evaluating the costs before making a decision? Inner strength as steadiness and forbearance?

Winds of Misfortune: Trust and Mistrust

Odysseus' ship rejoins the others. They set sail again. Their next stop is Aiolia Island where the wind king, Aiolos, is a gracious host. Odysseus tells him the tale of Troy, and in return, the wind king bottles the storm winds in a bag so that Odysseus can return safely home. Odysseus doesn't tell his men what is in the bag but guards it himself. After ten days, Ithaca is on the horizon—almost home at last.

Odysseus is very tired and falls asleep. Unaware of what

actually is in the bag, his crew open it, expecting to find gold and silver. The winds come roaring out at hurricane force and blow the ships back to Aiolia. The wind king is shocked that Odysseus is back again. He refuses to help him a second time and orders him out of his house as an "enemy of the gods."[4]

We ask ourselves, Have I ever allowed myself not to be awake at a moment that was critical for me to be alert? Have I ever been so driven by curiosity or greed that I have done something foolish to my detriment?

The deeper lesson of this episode is trust. Odysseus doesn't trust his men enough to tell them what is in the bag. They let their curiosity and greed get the better of trusting his instructions. Through mistrust, they all lose.

Entrapped by Circe: Lessons of Greed, Lack of Caution and the Power of Passion

After losing all but one ship to the man-eating giants of the land of the Laistrygonians, Odysseus and his surviving shipmates continue their homeward voyage. When they come to the island of the goddess Circe. Odysseus' men discover Circe's house and accept her hospitality.

She offers them posset, a drink of hot milk curdled with wine, sweetened and spiced. Alas, the drink is drugged with a magic potion! As soon as the men unsuspectingly swallow it, they lose all memory of their homeland and turn into swine. Their greed has come full circle. Circe adds insult to injury as she herds them into pigpens with a tap of her wand.

Only the one man who didn't enter Circe's house remains. He runs back to the ship, tells Odysseus what has happened, and begs him to leave the island right away. But Odysseus determines to try to save his men.

On his way to Circe's house, Odysseus meets Hermes, messenger of the gods. Hermes gives him a magic herb, moly, to protect him from Circe's spell and instructs Odysseus to draw his sword and rush at Circe as though to kill her when she tries to tap him with her wand. Hermes also tells him to make Circe take a vow to the gods that she will never attempt evil against him.

Odysseus follows Hermes' instructions to the letter. Sure enough, Circe invites him to come in and mixes him a drugged posset. He drinks it, but he has eaten the moly. Nothing happens. Circe taps him with her magic wand and orders him to the pigsty. Odysseus leaps up with sword drawn as though to kill her. She is shocked and dismayed that she cannot bewitch him. She realizes he is the famed Odysseus, "the man who is never at a loss."[5]

She invites him to make love to her, but he first makes her swear she will do no more harm and that she will turn his shipmates back into men. She agrees, and he and his men end up staying on the island with Circe. She treats them well, but they are no closer to home.

We ask ourselves, Have I ever allowed myself to be entrapped when I knew intuitively I should have exercised caution? Have I allowed my desires or passions to rule me, to detain me from pursuing my destiny?

Surviving the Sirens: Flirting with Recklessness

After a year has passed, Odysseus' men plead with him to return home and Circe finally agrees. She instructs Odysseus to plug his oarsmen's ears with beeswax before they pass by the Sirens lest they all be lured to their deaths by the sorceresses' sweet songs. If Odysseus wants to listen he must have his men lash him to the mast and order them not to untie him no matter how much he cries out for them to do so. Otherwise, he will perish.

As they pass the Sirens, Odysseus demands that his crew untie him. This time they are obedient and do not do so. The ship makes it safely past the Sirens.

We ask ourselves, Do I ever let myself be enticed into situations that are potentially dangerous? Do I ever have the temptation to flirt recklessly with my passions? Is it worth the price if I lose self-control?

Scylla and Kharybdis: Caught Between a Rock and a Hard Place

Now Odysseus and his crew must pass Scylla and Kharybdis. Circe has warned him that he will have to sail between a rock and a whirlpool where they will meet two female monsters. Scylla at the rock has twelve flapping feet and six heads, each with a triple row of teeth. Kharybdis, the whirlpool monster, sucks everything down and spews it back up three times a day.

Circe advises Odysseus to hug the cliffs of Scylla even though she will take six of his men. Otherwise, he will lose the entire crew to the whirlpool monster. Odysseus asks if there is any way to fight off Scylla. Circe answers sharply that he is a hothead who is always asking for trouble, that Scylla is an immortal fiend and he will not do well to set himself against the gods. She tells him, in this awful dilemma, "flight is better than fight."[6]

Odysseus passes this test as he hugs the cliffs and doesn't fight Scylla, but the monster swallows up six of his men. He mourns this awful scene as the worst loss he has suffered yet on his fateful voyage, perhaps because in this situation he felt forced to make the decision that directly caused the brutal deaths of six shipmates.

We ask ourselves, Have I ever been between a rock and a hard place and had to accept the lesser of two evils? Have I ever had to cut my losses and move on even though it was extremely painful? How do I choose the high road in a situation of fight or flight?

Mutiny on the Island of Helios: The Inevitable Results of Rebellion and Giving In

Odysseus now comes to the island of Helios and orders his shipmates to shun the island. However, the men are weary, angry and mutinous. They insist on disembarking, which both Circe and Tiberius, the blind prophet in Hades, have warned Odysseus not to do. Odysseus finally gives in but warns that they must not harm Helios's cattle. They swear they won't.

Odysseus and his men end up marooned on the island

for a month. They try to live on fish and birds but are half starved. Finally the inevitable happens with this fearful, rebellious crew. When Odysseus slips away from his men to pray for help, the gods put him into a deep sleep during which the men kill some of the cattle. When he awakens to the smell of roasting meat, Odysseus is horrified to realize what they have done. But it is too late.

Helios demands restitution for his lost cattle or else he will go to the underworld and no longer will the sun light the earth. In response, Zeus strikes Odysseus' ship with a lightning bolt that breaks it into splinters. The ship is destroyed and only Odysseus survives.

We ask ourselves, Have I ever allowed myself to give in to something a friend begged me to do even though I knew it was wrong? Have I ever been so at the mercy of my desires that I risked destruction to fulfill them? What lessons have I learned?

Alone, Humbled and Helped by the Gods

Now Odysseus is on his own with a makeshift raft, which he floats back through Kharybdis and Scylla. As the whirlpool sucks in water and his raft, Odysseus clings to a bough of a fig tree and waits for Kharybdis to spit up the raft. When she does, he pulls himself onto it, lies flat and rows with his hands past Scylla.

He says, "The Father of gods and men would not allow her to set eyes on me, or I should not have escaped with my life."[7] He is learning humility.

We ask ourselves, Do I wait for a life-threatening situation before humbling myself before my God?

Seven Years of Testing with the Goddess Calypso

Odysseus drifts upon the open sea for nine days until he reaches the island of the beautiful goddess Calypso. Calypso wants Odysseus to marry her in return for immortality. Although he refuses marriage, he has no way to get off the island without her good will and help.

Calypso is loving and caring to Odysseus but insists that he lie with her at night in her cave. He spends his days sitting on the rocky shore, staring out to sea, eyes blinded with tears, thinking of Penelope and his lost men. He remains on the island for seven years.

Athena pleads with Zeus to save Odysseus. Zeus relents and sends Hermes to tell Calypso to send Odysseus home. The nymph tries once more to convince Odysseus to stay with her, but finally helps him build a raft and gives him food and water to sail home.

We ask ourselves, Have I ever gotten myself trapped in a karmic entanglement and been in such depths of despair that only the intervention of my God delivered me?

Final Leg of the Homeward Voyage: "Swim for It!"

Odysseus is not yet home free. Poseidon is still angry with him and whips up a storm that leaves him half-drowned and spinning around on his raft. The White Sea Goddess, Ino, takes pity upon Odysseus. She tells him to forsake the raft and swim, wearing only the veil she gives him around his waist. While he has the veil, he will not drown or come to harm. She gives him the veil and dives back into the sea.

As a parting thrust Poseidon brings up a huge wave that completely breaks up Odysseus' raft. He is left clinging to a single beam. Laying aside his doubts, he strips off his clothes and swims for shore, using Ino's veil.

Once on shore, through Athena's intercession, Nausicaä, daughter of the ruler of Phaiacia, takes pity on Odysseus. After hearing his story of woe and misadventures, the ruler of the Phaiacians sends a ship to take Odysseus back to Ithaca. He is home at last.

We may ask ourselves, Have I ever been confronted with such peril that my only choice as a naked soul was to humbly throw myself upon the mercy of God? How may I apply this lesson in my daily life?

Odysseus Has Learned His Lessons: He Bows to the Guidance of the Higher Feminine

Odysseus has learned his lessons. Even when Athena, disguised as a shepherd, tests him to reveal his identity or to betray his emotion upon coming home, Odysseus is cautious and ingenious. He even invents a tall tale about how he happened to come to Ithaca.

Athena is pleased. She reveals to Odysseus who she is and tells him what has been happening in his palace. One hundred and eight suitors have tried to win the hand of Penelope. They have taken over Odysseus' palace, helping themselves to his cattle and provisions and feasting every night at his expense.

Penelope has skillfully held the suitors off through the pretext of having to weave a shroud for Odysseus' aging father, which she never finishes. Each night for three years she has unwound the weaving she did the day before. However, the suitors have caught on to her ruse and are pressing her for a decision.

Odysseus says he will take on the suitors if the goddess Athena is with him. Psychologically, he is claiming partnership with the divine mentoring nature of the Higher Feminine, which Athena represents, in order to win his victory. Athena then transforms him into an old beggar dressed in rags so he will not be recognized. Odysseus accepts his humble appearance and carries out Athena's directives.

We ask ourselves, Do I understand the importance of balancing my heroic masculine self by partnering with the intuitive mentoring of my higher feminine nature? Do I put inner purpose ahead of my surface appearance? Do I exercise humility in pursuing my destiny?

Reunion of Father and Son:
The Patience and Humility of Odysseus Tested

Athena arranges for Telemachos to return to Ithaca from Pylos, where he has gone to seek the whereabouts of his father. At the right time, she reveals to him that the seeming beggar is Odysseus returned. After a joyful reunion, they plan how Odysseus will deal with the suitors and regain his kingdom. Odysseus bides his time even when he suffers taunts and insults from the suitors.

We ask ourselves, Do I have the patience to wait for the right moment to take action? Have I developed the inner character to accept a humble position? Can I resist the temptation to retaliate, to seek vengeance? Do I trust in God to show me how to deal with my adversaries?

Odysseus Reclaims His Palace and Kingdom: The Slaying of the Suitors

Penelope challenges the suitors to shoot Odysseus' great bow. She offers to marry the one who can shoot an arrow through the holes of twelve ax heads lined up. No one can do it. They can't even string the bow.

On Apollo's feast day, a faithful old servant carries the bow to Odysseus, who is still disguised as the beggar. To the amazement of the suitors, he easily strings it and shoots the arrow through the twelve ax heads. He strips off his rags and reveals himself as Odysseus, king of Ithaca.

The battle is on. Odysseus, his son and two other men, with the help of Athena foiling the suitors' shots, put the wastrel suitors to death. Athena has put Penelope into a deep sleep so she will not have to see the battle.

We ask ourselves, Do I have the wisdom to recognize intruders in the house of my being? Do I have the will and determination to slay any darkness in my inner house? Do I have the courage to go for it, no matter the odds, when the chips are down and it is the right thing to do?

The Reunion of Odysseus and Penelope

Once the battle is over the nurse runs upstairs to Penelope to tell her that Odysseus has returned and the suitors are dead. Wise Penelope does not immediately believe it, although she longs for it to be true.

She tests Odysseus until he responds to her with their personal secret, one only the two of them know—how he made their bed all of one piece, carved out of a live olive tree that is still rooted to the ground. She accepts him with joy as she realizes that he is indeed her beloved Odysseus returned. Thus, both Odysseus and Penelope have earned their loving reunion.

We ask ourselves, Have I claimed the redemption of my masculine and feminine qualities and thereby readied myself for a loving reunion with my divine consort? If not, what do I still need to redeem?

Odysseus Claims the Nobility of True Manhood

Odysseus seeks out his father, Laërtês, who lives in the country on a little farm. Great is the joy of their reunion. Athena arranges for the pacifying of feuds and the stopping of bloodshed on Ithaca. Odysseus' last lesson in Homer's tale is to refrain from further killing.

Athena admonishes him to "make an end of war and conflict"[8] and tells him to give honor to Zeus, the Father, highest of the gods. Odysseus obeys. As he claims the nobility of true manhood, his warring and strife end, once and for all.

We ask ourselves, Am I willing to do what it takes to bring peace to the warring parts of myself and to make peace with my God? Am I willing to make peace with my outer "enemies" as well?

Soul-Transformation and Self-Transcendence: Ever So Much More a Man and a King

Homer's Odysseus moves step-by-step through the process of self-transformation and transcendence as he faces one dramatic adventure after another in order to return home to Penelope. He learns and matures as he trusts the guidance of his mentor, Athena, and stands on his own two feet.

Odysseus has many opportunities to discern right from wrong, truth from deception. He experiences the sad results of his impulsiveness and cockiness and learns to exercise forbearance, to think before he speaks or acts. He learns to trust only the best in himself and to be cautious and watchful of his weaknesses.

He is ever so much more of a man and a king once he has transformed his weaknesses and redeemed his lower nature. He earns the right to reunion with faithful Penelope, who represents his feminine qualities and the true desires of his soul.

We, too, may restore our masculine side to true nobility by honing strength of character, integrity of heart and a "can-do" spirit. Our feminine, our soul, will keep pace if we are wise, loving and faithful to our highest dreams and aspirations. Thus we set the stage for the alchemical union of soul and Spirit, and reunion with our twin soul—wherever he or she may be.[9]

What will be the outcome of our personal odyssey of self-transformation? It is up to us. As we pursue self-mastery, inner strength and tender heartedness, we too may win the victory of our Selfhood.

Your Personal Odyssey
of Transformation

1. *Take some time to outline the major points of serious challenges you have experienced in your life.*

2. *Look at each one of these experiences as though you were Odysseus and this were one of your major tests. What have you learned?*

3. *How have these challenges transformed your character?*

4. *Are you applying what you have learned to your life today? In what way?*

5. *How may the character you are forging help you to create a better tomorrow?*

6. *What do you perceive as the qualities and strengths of your masculine side? How might you develop these more strongly to complement and enhance your feminine?*

CHAPTER SEVEN

Soul Lessons: The Quest of Our Inner Heroine

Somewhere over the rainbow
Bluebirds fly.
Birds fly over the rainbow—
Why, then, oh why can't I?
—DOROTHY IN *THE WIZARD OF OZ*

*L*et's look at another travel adventure, a modern tale of self-transcendence. This time we will explore the lessons of our soul and the transformation of our feminine side as we follow the adventures of Dorothy in the timeless movie, *The Wizard of Oz*.[1] Each of the characters offers a gift to assist us in our transformational process.

As you remember, Dorothy lives with her Uncle Henry and Aunt Em on their farm in Kansas. They are good, hardworking folk who of necessity put chores first. Dorothy's best friend is her rambunctious little dog, Toto.

As our story opens, Toto has created a big problem. Dorothy is very angry and worried that the crabby neighbor, Miss Gulch, is going to do something bad to Toto because he got into her garden, chased her cat and bit her when she hit him with a rake. However, everyone is much too busy with chores to listen to Dorothy's troubles.

Aunt Em just tells her, "Find yourself a place where you won't get into any trouble." So Dorothy daydreams and sings to herself about a beautiful place somewhere over the rainbow—where there aren't any troubles, and dreams come true. However, trouble comes riding in with Miss Gulch on her bicycle and a notice from the sheriff that Toto is to be put away because he bit Miss Gulch. Over

Dorothy's tearful protests, Miss Gulch rides off with Toto in a basket.

When Toto jumps out and comes home, Dorothy decides the only way to save him is to run away with him. She meets up with Professor Marvel, a good man and traveling magician, who wisely looks into his crystal ball and tells her that Aunt Em is crying for her.

Dorothy goes running back home, but not in time. A twister is touching down, and everyone has gone into the storm cellar. It's too late when Dorothy gets there, so she seeks shelter in the house. As a window blows out, a piece of wood hits her on the head—and our adventure begins.

Dorothy is flung into another world, the world of her fears, her hopes and dreams. As her house whirls through the air, Miss Gulch blows by riding her bicycle and turns into a witch on a broom—revealing her inner witchy nature. The house finally comes down with a big bump in the "somewhere over the rainbow" land of the Munchkins.

The Gifts of Our Own Inner Characters— In Kansas and the Land of the Munchkins

We will be looking at the characters in this modern fairy tale on two levels: 1) as inner parts of Dorothy who contribute to her transformational journey, and 2) as inner parts of ourselves whose transformation fulfills our quest for freedom of our soul and spirit.

The drama, therefore, represents our own inner world as well as Dorothy's, and Dorothy herself represents our soul, our heroine. Thus, this tale is about our soul's quest for her* higher destiny. All of the characters portray archetypal patterns of human nature, even as the events represent typical fears, hopes and dreams. As we shall see, each character and event offers us a special gift in our own transformational process.

On the human level of our soul's journey, Dorothy can be seen as our inner girl child,[2] who is basically kindhearted and somewhat naïve. She has a bit of underlying temper that comes quickly to the surface when she is defending someone she loves, but she really can't bear cruelty of any kind. Her longing for a beautiful place where "there isn't any trouble" sets the stage for her inner transformational adventure.

Whether man or woman, do we recognize the girl child within? Do we recognize our soul peeping through her eyes, envisioning a world of beauty and freedom beyond the seeming dreariness of everyday life? Our soul as the inner girl child brings the gifts of innocence and warmheartedness. Yet she needs to learn to deal with unpleasant realities instead of getting angry or running away.

Toto represents the loyal but uninhibited part of ourselves. Although he is Dorothy's best friend, he is also a rambunctious bundle of curiosity. And he doesn't hesitate to bite back if someone is mean to him. He offers the gift

---

*The soul is referred to as "she" or "her" because each soul, in man or woman, is the feminine counterpart of Spirit. The soul is also the essence of the "inner feminine," even as the spirit (lowercased) is the essence of the "inner masculine" and referred to as "he" or "him."

of friendship and devotion but hasn't learned nonreactivity and dependability. Do we recognize this part of ourselves that gets us into trouble sometimes?

Aunt Em and Uncle Henry personify archetypal patterns of love expressed through dedication to hard work and down-to-earth practicality. They offer us the gifts of constancy and perseverance. Yet they need Dorothy's warmheartedness and Toto's instinctive exuberance to balance their hardworking, serious nature. Do we recognize the Uncle Henry and Aunt Em parts of ourselves? Do we persevere in what we set out to do? Is our constancy and perseverance balanced with warmheartedness and exuberance?

The farmhouse represents the living space of our inner family in a rather desolate area of Kansas. In this drama, we are called to bring beauty to the inner house of our being rather than trying to find it outside of ourselves.

The cyclone itself may be seen as the underlying turmoil of Dorothy's inner emotions that are capable of spinning her around and turning her topsy-turvy, sending her crashing into a different world.

Thus the stage is set for Dorothy and Toto to fly far away to the beautiful land of Dorothy's dreams "somewhere over the rainbow." We may ask ourselves, Do I have underlying emotional turmoil that at times reaches cyclonic proportions? Where will it take me? What am I meant to learn?

The gift of the cyclone is that even as it brings whirling

change, it also brings transformation. Do we welcome the gift of transformational change?

Dorothy and Toto whirl through the air in the farmhouse until they land with a thud in the Land of the Munchkins. This quaint and colorful land fulfills the inner girl child's dream of beauty and fairy-tale charm, yet a sense of "home" is missing. And there are those two Wicked Witches, signifying witchy Miss Gulch as "double trouble."

Dorothy's tendency to temper is reflected back to her in Miss Gulch's generally angry nature and controlling ways. In Dorothy's "dream," Miss Gulch first turns into the Wicked Witch of the East, symbolizing her abuse of power through angry hatred and evil tyranny. Thus, the Witch has cruelly tyrannized the Munchkins, who represent Dorothy's fearful parts—and our own.

Dorothy's house lands on the Wicked Witch of the East, killing her and leaving only her ruby slippers, which symbolize Dorothy's opportunity for freedom to return home—although she doesn't know it yet. The deep ruby color symbolizes an intensity of fiery love that can be expressed either as divine love or as intense hatred, depending on the character of the one who possesses it.

Once the dark side of hateful, evil tyranny in the person of the Wicked Witch of the East is vanquished, Dorothy is free for a little while to explore the Land of the Munchkins as her happy world that offers beauty and natural healing. Now that Dorothy has freed the Munchkins from the Witch, both Dorothy and the Munchkin people may reclaim their carefree, childlike nature.

Are you in bondage to any form of inner tyranny, such as anger, hatred or underlying fears that come from your negative shadow side? Do you realize that you also have an inner carefree nature? Do you nurture this gentle, innocent part of yourself?

With the death of the Wicked Witch of the East, angry hatred and abject fear (two major elements in need of transformation) have been partly resolved. We shall see how they are to be further transformed through the rest of Dorothy's journey in the Land of Oz.

Glinda, the beautiful Good Witch of the North, appears to Dorothy and the Munchkins and magically transfers the ruby slippers onto Dorothy's feet. She tells Dorothy that she must never take them off or she will be at the mercy of the Wicked Witch of the West—who is even more evil than her sister witch.

Glinda offers the gift of guidance and new direction, the start of a new cycle, as she instructs Dorothy to "follow the yellow brick road" to ask the Wizard of Oz for help. She also gives Dorothy a kiss of protection. Do you listen to your wise Higher Feminine when she offers you new direction? Do you accept the protection her wisdom bestows upon you?

Since the yellow brick road represents down-to-earth illumination, we know Dorothy is to pursue illumined, yet practical, understanding on her transformational journey. As she sets off wearing her ruby slippers, we may ask ourselves,

Am I following the yellow brick road of golden illumination and down-to-earth understanding in my life? How might I claim my own ruby slippers of love and freedom?

Inner Lessons from Dorothy's Companions: Scarecrow, Tin Man and Cowardly Lion

Dorothy meets her next redemptive character in the Scarecrow perched on a pole in the middle of a field. The Scarecrow feels he is a failure because he can't scare the crows. He longs to have the brains of a real man, and when he finds out that Dorothy is going to the Emerald City, he decides to go with her and see if the Wizard will give him brains.

It is interesting to note that all the way through this movie, it is usually the Scarecrow who figures everything out, yet he has no confidence in himself because he *thinks* he hasn't any brains. He represents the part of ourselves who acts "brainless" but does so out of a lack of confidence in our own intuitive thinking.

Do you recognize the Scarecrow part of yourself who firmly believes you need more intellect, more brains? Are you overlooking the gift of wisdom that comes in the form of your intuition and inner knowing?

As the inner journey of our soul continues, Dorothy and the Scarecrow discover the Tin Man rusted in position, holding his ax in the air. With the Scarecrow helping her, Dorothy compassionately oils the Tin Man's joints until he can turn his head, lower his ax and move his arms and legs.

He explains that one day when he went out to chop

wood, the rain came and he rusted in place. He tells Dorothy that he feels very empty inside because the tinsmith forgot to give him a heart. He doesn't believe he registers emotion, nor that he can love. Dorothy suggests that the Tin Man go with them to the Emerald City to ask the Wizard for a heart.

The curious thing about the Tin Man is that he is the one who is so tenderhearted that he is often moved to tears out of love and concern for the others. It is the Tin Man who actually offers the gift of a tender heart.

Thus, the Tin Man represents an aspect of ourselves that is deluded into thinking we cannot love, even when we clearly express tenderheartedness. Once again, it is a lack of confidence. We lack confidence that we have what it takes to love because we believe our heart is broken or has been stolen from us.

Do you recognize the part of yourself that lacks confidence in your capacity to love? Do you recognize the true gift of love you offer when you express tenderness and compassion to others?

Off they go to see the Wizard, a threesome now, as they make their way through a forest and come upon the Cowardly Lion. Now, the lion is supposed to be "the king of the jungle." But this Lion is all bluster and bluff. Underneath he is quivering with fear. When he goes after Toto, the smallest of the group, Dorothy slaps the Lion, and he bursts into tears. He admits he's a coward, a big sissy. Dorothy and her friends suggest he come with them to see the Wizard.

The Cowardly Lion decides he will go with them to the Emerald City to ask the Wizard for courage, although he trembles with fear at the prospect. Yet throughout the rest of the tale, we realize that it is the Cowardly Lion who takes the greatest risks because to do anything at all he has to overcome paralyzing fear.

The Cowardly Lion brings the gift of courage, which means to behave courageously even when you are scared. When the chips are down and Dorothy's life is at stake, he does just that. Thus, the Cowardly Lion represents a part of us that doesn't have confidence in our courage even when we behave courageously. He's also the part of us that tends to cover our fear with bluster and bluff and at the same time with perhaps a tinge of pride!

Are you aware of the part of you that doesn't have confidence in your courage? Are you aware of the gift you offer when you choose to protect yourself or others or to forge ahead in spite of scary circumstances?

Each one of the three characters symbolizing different aspects of our masculine side lacks confidence. What does this lack of confidence represent? At its root, it comes down to fear—the Scarecrow fears he's brainless, the Tin Man fears he's heartless, and the Cowardly Lion fears he's a coward. Dorothy, our girl child, also has fear—the fear that she will never be able to return home to Aunt Em.

Why does Dorothy have these companions? They reflect aspects of her unredeemed masculine that she, as the inner girl child aspect of our soul, needs to be able to trust.

*As we transform brainlessness, heartlessness and fearfulness into
wisdom, strength of heart and courage, our masculine spirit
emerges as a balance to the intuitive, compassionate, innocent
nature of our soul.*

Ask yourself, Do I mistrust my inner wisdom, forget to
trust my heart or find myself wanting to run from challenging circumstances? If any of this applies, you have found
your own inner Scarecrow, Tin Man and Cowardly Lion.

Also ask yourself, Do I keep looking somewhere else to
be "at home" instead of putting my roots down wherever
I am and knowing that home is where my heart is? If the
answer is yes, you have found your inner Dorothy. All of
these characters within await the transformational process.

The Field of Desires, "Do-It-Yourself" Wizardry, and The Challenge of the Power of Evil

Although every aspect of this fairy tale may be viewed as
transformational, we will look only at the high points. On
the way to the Emerald City, the deadly poppy field almost
does in the Lion, Dorothy and Toto. The poppy field represents the opium of inordinate desires, which gradually
puts the vulnerabilities of the flesh to sleep—much like the
Lotus-eaters in the Odyssey and Pinocchio's forgetfulness
in the face of various seductions. Until our human vulnerabilities are transformed, we are vulnerable to the ploys of
the negative shadow side.

The Wicked Witch of the West, who is following our
travelers everywhere they go, has put the opium spell on

the poppies to get her revenge and to try to steal Dorothy's ruby slippers. The Lion, Dorothy and Toto all succumb to the spell and fall asleep in the field. But Glinda, the Good Witch of the North, hears the Scarecrow and Tin Man calling for help. She brings a purifying snowstorm that stops the poisonous effect of the poppies and wakes up the Lion, Dorothy and Toto.

When the travelers arrive at the Emerald City, they see the glittering city as many beautiful shades of green. Why? Green is the color of nature, of healing and truth. Thus we understand the metaphor that healing is in process but it will come through envisioning their inner capacity for transformation and staying true to their higher nature.

The Wicked Witch has followed the travelers and writes *Surrender Dorothy* in the sky. The heat is now on for Dorothy and her companions, and when they knock on the door to see the Wizard, he at first refuses to see them. When he finally agrees to do so, he appears as a huge head, with smoke and fire around him. He proceeds to insult them until Dorothy finally stands up to him. Then he says that he will help them, but first they must prove themselves worthy by bringing him the broomstick of the Wicked Witch of the West.

What is the gift of this terrible Wizard? His wizardry is a do-it-yourself plan. Rather than looking for a magical solution, each one must conquer his or her fear of the Wicked Witch's hatred and anger through strength of will, sharpness of mind, compassion of heart and unswerving dedication to purpose.

Thus we ask ourselves, Do I have a tendency to expect magic or to look outside myself for solutions? If so, we need to ask our Higher Self to illumine us and to help us claim the will, the mind and the heart to resolve our problems and fulfill the destiny of our soul.

So off go the travelers, frightened but trying to mobilize their courage. The Wicked Witch of the West plagues them by magically lifting the Tin Man up in the air and dropping him, which bangs him up a bit. She throws fire at the Scarecrow, which is the only thing that really scares him. The Cowardly Lion is already so scared that she doesn't bother much with him. She finally sends her Winged Monkeys, who terrify them all. They take the straw out of the Scarecrow and fly back to the Witch's castle carrying Dorothy and Toto.

With Dorothy cheering him on, Toto manages to run away and get out of the castle. He goes to find the Tin Man, Scarecrow and Cowardly Lion and leads them back to the Witch's castle. They drum up their mutual courage to try to rescue Dorothy. The Scarecrow comes up with a plan, the Tin Man agrees, and the Cowardly Lion finally comes along, for Dorothy's sake.

Three of the Witch's guards surprise the trio, but they get the best of the guards and march into the castle disguised in uniform. Toto leads them to where Dorothy is locked in a room, and the Tin Man chops down the door just as the hourglass of life is running out for her. They do battle with the Witch and her guards but are finally trapped and surrounded. Now they are face-to-face with the power of evil in the Wicked Witch of the West. What kind of miracle will it take?

Ask yourself, How do I muster the courage and faith to confront the power of darkness within myself or another? Do I remember to ask God for a miracle?

Lessons and Gifts from the Dissolution of the Wicked Witch of the West

The Wicked Witch is determined to kill Dorothy, because as long as Dorothy is alive she can't get her ruby slippers. She is going to do away with all of them, starting with the Scarecrow. But when she sets the Scarecrow on fire, Dorothy bravely douses the fire with a bucket of water and the water splashes on the Witch. Screaming, "I'm melting, I'm melting," she melts into the nothingness that she really is, and all of the guards hail Dorothy and give her the Witch's broomstick to take back to the Wizard of Oz.

Actually, the scary Wicked Witch of the West was nothing but an emotional coward behind all her shrewish blustering and bullying. She represents fear, hatred, deceit and the cruelty of a raging ego, all of which melt into nothingness when confronted with the courage and caring for one another demonstrated by Dorothy and her friends.

We may ask ourselves, Do I recognize anything of that emotional, shrewish, bullying feminine in me? If so, we can decide to dissolve that inner witch. Purity of intention, purity of conscience, purity of loving action—these are gifts of the brave, loving feminine that melt the witch consciousness.

Dorothy's melting of the Wicked Witch is also the final dissolution of her own inner fear and anger, which is being replaced by the courage and fortitude it has taken for her to turn her journey into a transformational victory. Do we daily attempt to transform our fear and anger into courage and inner strength?

The guards represent the helplessness of the slave consciousness. They have to be rescued from the witchy emotional tyrant before they can lose their fear and come into their own. We may ask ourselves, Am I a slave to certain fearsome thoughts, emotions or habits that bully me? How do I heal my knee-jerk, emotional reactions?

First, we can choose to replace our subconscious mental scare tactics with wisdom and hope. Second, we can lovingly soothe ourselves when we feel scared. Third, we may mobilize strength of heart to take firm, positive action. By giving that fear the good old "one, two, three" punch of courage, we replace it with a gentle sense of fearlessness. Try it. It works!

Encounters with the Humbug Wizard of Oz

When our heroine and her companions arrive once again at the Emerald City, they tell the Keeper of the Gate that Dorothy has melted the Wicked Witch of the West and they have returned for the Wizard of Oz to fulfill his promises. Once again they stand before the huge head with its fire and smoke.

When the Wizard does not immediately respond to their request for him to fulfill his promises, instinctive Toto goes exploring and pulls the curtain open where the Wizard is standing. There stands the great Wizard of Oz, a short man with a bald head and round face. He admits that he is a humbug Wizard, who originally came to Oz by balloon from Omaha, Nebraska. Do we recognize our own tendency to be a humbug at times? Do we ever try to fake our way through tough situations?

The Wizard says that even though he is a humbug Wizard he is a good man and will give the Lion, Scarecrow and Tin Man their courage, brains and heart. But he will have to think about how to help Dorothy get back to Kansas.

The Wizard tells the Scarecrow that he has as many brains as learned people, but the one thing he does not have is a diploma. So he gives him a beautiful diploma with the honorary degree of Th.D., Doctor of Thinkology, which certainly attests to his wisdom. The Scarecrow can't thank him enough and now feels very wise indeed.

Next, the Wizard tells the Cowardly Lion that he is simply a victim of disorganized thinking, that he has as much courage as any hero. But the one thing he does not have is a medal to show for it. So the Wizard gives the Lion a medal for meritorious conduct, extraordinary valor and conspicuous bravery and makes him a member of the Legion of Courage. The Lion immediately feels filled with courage. He also expresses his gratitude to the Wizard.

Finally, the Wizard tells the Tin Man that while the hearts of "good-deed doers" are no bigger than his, the one thing he does not have is a testimonial. In consideration of the Tin Man's kindness, he gives him a testimonial, a heart-shaped clock that ticks, which the Tin Man attaches to his chest. He is very happy to have such a wonderful heart and thanks the Wizard for his kindness.

Thus, the Wizard gives the Scarecrow, Lion and Tin Man physical symbols of qualities they have already developed. Of course, the Wizard knew he would be able to give these three what they wanted because they imagined he could do anything. But it will take more than imagination to get Dorothy home to Kansas.

He decides to launch the hot-air balloon that brought him to Oz in the first place. He and Dorothy will return to Kansas, which is not so far from Omaha, his hometown. He is tired of being a humbug Wizard and kindhearted enough to want to help Dorothy return home. He appoints the Scarecrow, Tin Man and Lion to rule the Emerald City in his absence.

As the balloon fills with hot air, the Wizard, Dorothy and Toto get in and say goodbye to the people. All of a sudden Toto jumps out of Dorothy's arms and runs off. Before she can find him and climb back into the basket with the Wizard, the balloon rises into the air. The Wizard can't bring it back, and Dorothy is brokenhearted.

You see, the "humbug Wizard," who represents the cleverness of the human mind, is able to perform so-called wizardry only through someone else's naïve belief in the power of suggestion. He is not able to take our heroine all the way "home."

Dorothy must find a higher resolution through her steadfast determination to return home and through the loving guidance of Glinda, the Good Witch of the North.

The Ultimate Gift of Dorothy's Journey: The Loving Guidance of the Higher Feminine

As the Wizard disappears into the distant sky, the beautiful pink bubble reappears and gently settles to the ground in the Emerald City. To Dorothy's relief, out steps Glinda. She brings the gift of beauty of character and the loving understanding of the Higher Feminine. She solves problematic situations by the power, wisdom and love of the heart.

Ask yourself, Do I honor those higher qualities in myself that I see reflected in Glinda? Do I use my inner power to be courageous, wise, loving and forgiving? Do I claim the gifts of my soul's transformation through the qualities of the Higher Feminine?

Glinda lovingly tells Dorothy that she has always had the power to return home to Kansas through the ruby slippers, but that she wouldn't have believed it before going through her adventures in the Land of Oz.

Dorothy realizes that it wasn't enough to want to see Aunt Em and Uncle Henry. She had to realize that she always had her heart's desire right in her own backyard—

symbolically, within herself. Now she is ready to return home from her transformational journey. All she has to do is click her heels together three times and command the ruby slippers to carry her wherever she wishes to go.

We note that, metaphysically, the "feet" symbolize understanding;[3] the ruby shoes represent the intensity of divine love. Dorothy has matured in her understanding of the freeing power of her heart's love and is no longer the naïve and helpless girl child. She has united the innocence of her soul with an inner sense of freedom—the fruit of her experiences in the Land of Oz.

Dorothy, as our inner girl child (our soul) has also benefited from helping to bring out the wisdom of mind, strength of heart and courage of her masculine spirit, represented in her dream by the Scarecrow, Tin Man and Lion. She has come to realize she can't run away from her problems, that she will continue to have them until she finds inner resolution. She has traded in her temper for a can-do spirit. All this she has faced and resolved in her dreamland, the Land of Oz.

Having gone through her inner transformational journey, Dorothy is ready to return to conscious awareness. She returns home wiser, more loving, more empowered—free to be the fullness of who she really is.

Dorothy kisses her friends and Glinda goodbye, takes Toto in her arms and solemnly clicks her heels together three times, repeating, "There's no place like home." Instantly she is whirling through the air as the ruby shoes return her to awaken in her bed at home in Kansas where Aunt Em is anxiously bending over her.

The central message of the fairy tale is that through her adventures, Dorothy comes to realize that home is where her heart is—and her heart is anchored in the Kansas plains with Uncle Henry and Aunt Em.

We may ask ourselves, What does "home" mean to me? What is my gift of "home?" Home can mean many wonderful things, such as a safe haven, putting down roots wherever we go, being true to our heart and soul, being "at home" with friends and loved ones. In the sense of inner "homing," we return to our heart as a sacred center, where we contact divine love and fulfill the yearnings of our soul and spirit.

I believe that each of us has an inner homing instinct. We have special places on earth where we feel at home, and we feel the comfort of hearth and home when we make soul-to-soul and heart-to-heart contact with one another. Our "home" is also an inner place of peace and calm, our own inner lighthouse that guides us through the storms of transformational change.

Ultimately, each one of us may unite the higher qualities of our soul and spirit to return Home to the planes of Spirit. When we return to the heaven-world with our earthly mission accomplished, we will experience a sense of freedom from the burdens of the physical plane. Best of all, we will celebrate true freedom in the highest sense—the freedom to be *all of who we really are*. Truly there is no place like Home!

Exercise: Claiming Your Inner Freedom

1. *Take a moment to meditate upon your soul and visualize her as a powerful, wise and loving heroine.*

2. *What are the special qualities of your soul (feminine), e.g., spontaneity, intuitive understanding, joy, playfulness, compassion, devotion, endurance, etc.?*

3. *What are the special qualities of your spirit (masculine) that complement and enhance your soul, e.g., wisdom, inner strength, kindness, courage, fortitude, the can-do spirit, integrity, etc.?*

4. *How might you synchronize your soul qualities with the essence of your spirit in your daily life?*

5. *How may you claim your freedom to be who you really are when people around you display hardheartedness, intellectual guile or power plays?*

6. *How might you strengthen your sense of inner freedom on a daily basis?*

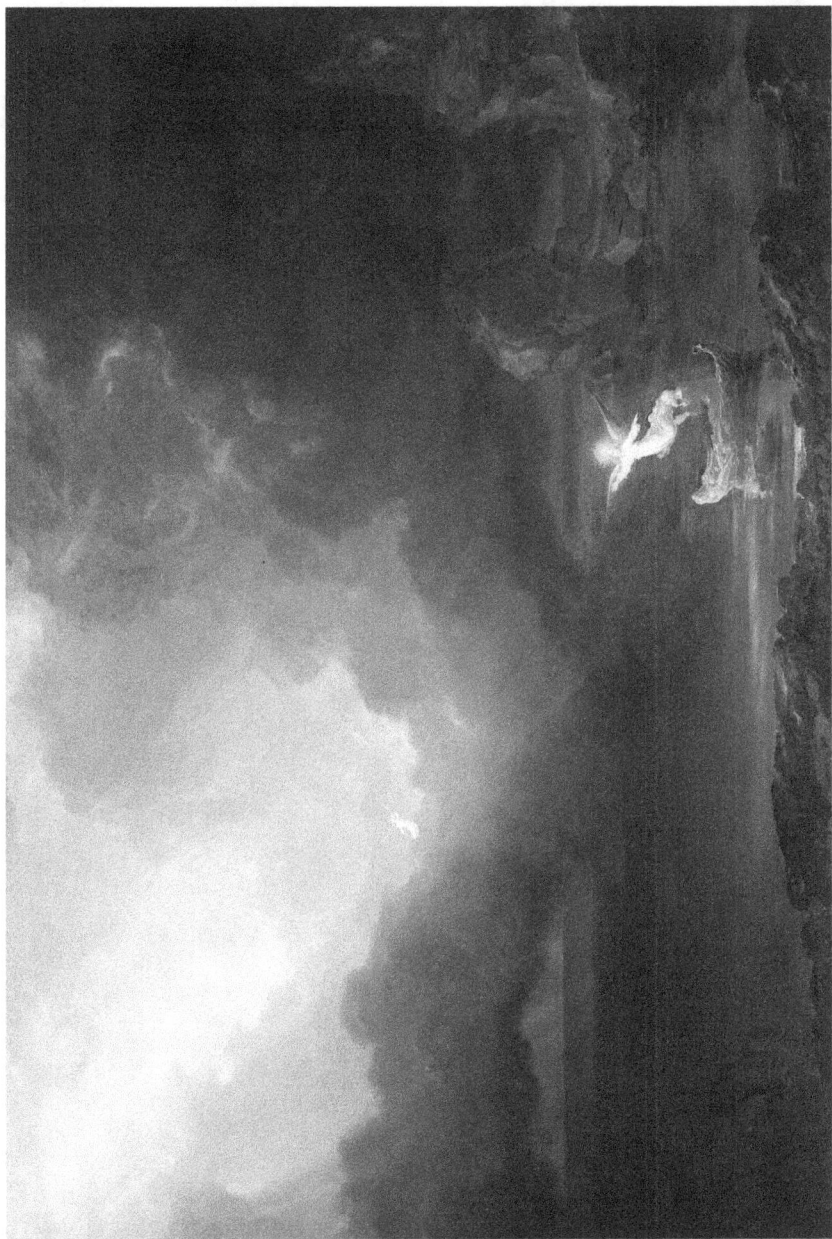

Thomas Cole, *The Voyage of Life: Old Age*. Alisa Mellon Fund, © 2000 Board of Trustees, National Gallery of Art, Washington.

CHAPTER EIGHT

The Inner Journey of Endings and Beginnings

To dry one's eyes and laugh at a fall,
And baffled, get up and begin again.

—ROBERT BROWNING

*A*vatars and mystics teach that each of us is meant to reawaken to who we are as beings of Universal Light. Many of us today are awakening to a sense of our destiny. Others remember coming from the heaven-world, "trailing clouds of glory,"[1] to fulfill a mission on earth. All of us are called to be living examples of divine love to show the way Home to brothers and sisters who have forgotten their origin. To do so, we must transcend the best and redeem the self-created worst in ourselves.

The Beginning of Beginnings and Endings: Claiming the Gift of "Who I Am"

When we leave the heaven-world to come into life on planet Earth, we say goodbye to brothers and sisters of light in the planes of Spirit. We feel the pain of separating from those we love, and we do not know when we will see one another again. During the nine months or so in the womb, we have a certain sense of oneness with our mother—and again the pain of separation when we are born. No wonder newborn babies cry.

Oneness and separation is the ebb and flow of life that moves with us all the way from the heaven-world through infancy, childhood and all succeeding stages of life. Each life experience has its beginning and that certain sense of loss that comes with the ending.

We feel the sense of loss as we leave the relative safety of the womb. We feel it again when we take our first steps away from mother, when we change schools, leave home for the first time, change jobs, say goodbye to someone we love, suffer a career setback, enter middle age or the senior years or undergo any other major change.

When we experience an ending and its accompanying sense of loss, we feel a sense of separateness and loneliness. Yet, the comforting lesson in the drama of separation is that when thrust on our own, we have a special opportunity to claim the jewels of our own being—our own vibration, our own thoughts, our own feelings, our own way of addressing life. The gift of separation is that particular joy of sensing, "This is me. This is who *I am!*"

When we come together with other people, there is another kind of jewel, a rainbow jewel that emerges from the synergy of the flow of our communication and interaction with one another.

As we remember, scientists are discovering through "chaos theory"[2] that nature evolves from within rather than from any structure that is imposed from without. This is how we grow and expand. We have our inner being that is God-given, the person we are as God created us to be. Our soul identity is clothed with a physical body when we enter life. With each new cycle of life we move from a sense of integration and oneness through the experience of separation and isolation into a new sense of oneness and integration.

We continually thrust ourselves into new times, places and experiences as we journey through life. Certain of these moments affirm who we inwardly know ourselves to be while other moments quarrel with us. When we find ourselves losing the quarrel, it is helpful to turn to our inner awareness and memories that remind us of who we are in the essence of our heart and soul.

Memories of Childhood and the Exciting Process of Individuation

I remember some of the times in my childhood when I experienced my essence, what I called "the Marilynness" of me. These were often secret alone times or good times with a special friend. I remember riding my bike for miles on Arizona's country roads, enjoying the shady trees, fragrant orange groves, a fountain here or there, children playing in the sprinklers, and special times like riding with my friend Virginia on her pony through the desert, drinking in the beauty of desert cactus blossoms and wildflowers in the spring.

Then there were those memorable summers on the beach in California where my sister and I would play and swim in the ocean, bury ourselves in the sand, roller skate on the boardwalk, ride the merry-go-round and reach for the gold ring that promised a free ride.

I loved to read. I often read on the school bus, even when getting on and off. No, I never fell on my face but

I came close! The characters from special books like Louisa May Alcott's *Little Women*, L. Frank Baum's *The Wizard of Oz* and Charles Sheldon's *In His Steps* were inner companions. I could lose myself in such books because they talked about what I thought or felt and thereby brought peace and comfort to my heart and soul. In the process of all of this I came more and more to know myself.

All of these experiences were a part of the exciting process that Carl Jung called "individuation,"³ the adventure of coming to know and claim the uniqueness of our individuality. I believe aloneness experiences help us to establish and affirm who we are and to envision all that we may become. We need time with ourselves to establish our sense of identity and to set our inner boundaries.

From that point of inner awareness we are ready to come out of separateness and aloneness into interaction with others, into friendships, into love relationships. When we enter relationships from a point of having already established our identity, we have more to offer. We are no longer simply an echo of everyone around us.

Cycles of Change and Self Discovery: Are You Living Your Life as an Echo?

Some people live a lot of their lives being echoes. Have you ever thought about that? They echo this, they echo that, they echo what they hear from this person, from that person, or on TV. We are not really happy and fulfilled as an echo.

Have you ever gone into a canyon and shouted and

heard the echo coming back at you? I remember doing this for the first time as a child in the Superstition Mountains in Arizona and being startled that someone was shouting back at me! It certainly expanded my consciousness and curiosity about how everything works to realize my own voice had gone out into space and was echoing back to me. (This was also a good lesson to me in a spiritual sense, of how everything we send out returns to us. It was an early precursor to my understanding of the law of karma.)

Whether by ourselves or with others, we want to go beyond being the echo of what happened a minute ago. We want to be who we are in the present. From this perspective, aloneness is a gift. When we reach up to hold God's hand and ask the angels to be with us in each of our life's dramas, we have precious moments of inner discovery and transformation as we pass through the cycles of change.

When you really think about it, every cycle of change and period of individuation is about self-discovery. It is an opportunity to reflect, to integrate the past and to allow ourselves to grow a little more. Of course, if we shut down when changes come, we don't grow. And life is all about growing; life is about becoming more and more of who we are and creating more and more of who we can become.

Creation is an ongoing process. Even our physical bodies form and reform over time. As Dr. Margaret Wheatley puts it:

"Although we experience ourselves as a stable form, our body changes frequently. As physician Deepak Chopra likes to explain, our skin is new every month, our liver every six weeks; and even our brain, with all those valuable cells storing acquired knowledge, changes its content of carbon, nitrogen, and oxygen about every twelve months. Day after day, as we inhale and exhale, we give off what were our cells, and take in elements from other organisms to create new cells. 'All of us,' observes Chopra, 'are much more like a river than anything frozen in time and space' (1990). In spite of this exchange, we remain rather constant, due to the organizing function of the *information* contained in our DNA."[4]

I believe that even as our cells change and renew on an ongoing basis, so do our souls have their own process of growth and renewal. To me, it's all about God becoming more of God as life at every level of creation changes and evolves.

Letting go of the old and taking hold of the new is an integral part of living a fruitful and fulfilling life. When we hold on instead of letting go, we pay a big price. Mentally, emotionally and physically we tie ourselves to the past instead of living in the present. Our souls feel stifled and unhappy.

Alive and Well in the Present, We Can Let Go and Move On

I will always remember Natasha, a client of mine in the 1970s. She was in her mid-thirties and came in for therapy because of the overly dependent relationship she still had with her mother, who was a woman in her early sixties.

Natasha told me she would not be able to bear it if anything happened to her mother. Her mother was actually in quite good health and was concerned about her daughter's dependency on her.

Natasha had been separated from her mother as a small child of about six. This was in Europe during World War II, when they were fleeing out of Hungary to escape the Nazi troops. She remembered how terrified she was that she would never see her mother again. She wanted to cry but knew she had to keep on moving with the others or she would die. A kind woman who had been a neighbor took her under her wing, and they made it across the border to safety. Within a few days, Natasha was reunited with her mother, who had also managed to cross the border.

She grew up but remained attached to her mother in a way that was uncomfortable for both of them. She had never forgotten that terrible experience. It was a childhood terror that had dogged her life ever since. As a woman of 37, she came to me for therapy because she realized she had to resolve her past both for her own sake and her mother's sake. She was still mourning the loss of her mother—who was actually alive and well.

In the course of therapy, Natasha came to realize that holding on to her fear of losing her mother had held her back from marrying and living a full life. I remember the day she made a major turnaround. We were doing inner-child work, and she went through that terrible childhood experience again. She discovered that her inner child still felt bereft and wanted to cling to her mother. Why? Because Natasha had not become the loving adult she needed to be to comfort and protect her own inner child.

Natasha worked hard on staying centered in her loving adult so she could comfort and reassure her inner child. At the end of several sessions, she began to realize that she was capable of mothering herself, that she did not need to continue to mourn the possibility of losing her mother.

She began to practice standing on her own two feet emotionally and making decisions without consulting her mother. As she made progress, her fear began to wane, and she started feeling excited about doing things on her own.

Several months later, Natasha's mother, Eva, came in for a follow-up session with her daughter. Eva was delighted at the progress Natasha had made. In that session it was as if the shroud that had covered their relationship suddenly disappeared. Natasha hugged her mother and told her how much she loved her and that she was ready to get on with her own life.

Eva hugged her back and heaved a huge sigh of relief. She said, "Little one, you will always be precious to me, but I am so glad you are growing up. I have worried about how attached you have been to me because I will not always be here. And that needs to be all right with you.

"I will always love you as my sweet child, but I have also looked forward to our having an adult friendship. Now it looks like we are going to make that happen. As to the future, I trust God and know that whatever is to come, both of us will be safe in His loving arms. Hasn't God always looked out for us and protected us?"

Natasha agreed, "Yes, I trust God, and I'm beginning to trust myself. I don't know what took me so long, but I'm determined to become a whole person. I am going to get on with my life." Her mother smiled and gave her another hug. Natasha was finally letting go.

Shortly after completing therapy, she married and in quick succession had two children of her own. She laughingly told me, "I am making up for lost time!" She also told me that her relationship with her mother was good and she no longer feared her mother dying. She knew she would miss her mother when she passed on, but she no longer anticipated the return of the terror and despair of her childhood.

She made a very touching comment: "It is so wonderful to be who I am as an adult. I love my husband and children so much. And they love me. Can you imagine that I remained a child of six for thirty years? Please tell anyone else who's stuck like I was that they *can* let go and move on. God will help them."

Is there any element of this life story that is yours as well? How often we perceive an old situation of scary loss as our present reality. When the mother is nowhere to be found, a little child definitely perceives himself or herself as abandoned, lost, all alone. Yet, as adults we can choose to let go of these childhood experiences and resolve the trauma of loss. We can leave the past behind, embrace the present and get on with our life.

Scenarios of Endings and Beginnings in the Whirl of Change

Today people everywhere in the world, particularly in scientific, corporate and high-tech arenas are experiencing the whirl of beginnings and endings. Our mobile society often necessitates leaving friends behind and making new ones. New discoveries push us to let go of old ways of thinking and doing. Many people have gone through a restructuring or reengineering of their job. Endings and beginnings seem to occur more often in our fast-paced societies. Facing change is not easy, but we grow from our experiences as we learn our lessons, look ahead and move on.

Have any of the above scenarios happened to you in the past few years? If so, how did you handle your feelings? It is important to look back on these times and remember what provided you a safety net that helped you stay afloat and the lessons you learned that strengthened you.

Are you claiming a new beginning and feeling good about yourself today? If not, what is holding you back?

If there is a cycle of change, ending or beginning, occurring in your life right now, I suggest that you take a good look at it and try to come to resolution with any underlying feelings. Otherwise, they may drain your energy even as you determine to move forward.

Ask yourself, What aspect of this situation do I still need to resolve? What are my feelings about it? Why is it bothering me? Is there a lesson I need to learn? Is holding on to the past keeping me from embracing today with the full gusto of my passion and capabilities? If so, am I willing and ready to let it go?

Check it out. Maybe you are lonely or disheartened after the breakup of a relationship or upset or discouraged about losing a job or a comfortable way of life. Perhaps you are feeling apprehensive about moving to a new location, saying goodbye to old friends and reaching out to new people. Or perhaps you are concerned about future financial stability. Most importantly, maybe you feel you haven't been true to yourself or you have somehow lost contact with your center.

You may be aware of only a nagging feeling, uncomfortable thought, or sense of unrest in your body that seems related to an ending or beginning in your life—past or present. Whatever has come to mind as you think about these possible scenarios is important to focus on as we continue to explore life as a voyage of transformation.

Renewed Opportunity Beyond Retirement

What about handling the retirement years? Not all people look forward to arbitrary retirement. Some of us decide we are never going to retire, no matter what happens. We are simply going to keep moving on and finding something new to do. My father, Russell Cooper, taught me that. He always kept pace with the cycles of life.

As a child, he moved with his family by covered wagon all the way from their farm in Louisville, Kentucky, to Deming, New Mexico, because of his health. My grandparents created a new business, a new home.

After my father married, he and my mother, my five-year-old sister and I as a two-year-old moved from Deming to Phoenix, Arizona, because of my sister's health. My father created a new business, a new home.

When my mother passed on, my father remarried and put together two families, with five children where we had been three. All his life my father kept moving with the cycles of change and renewal.

The day before he went into the hospital to have surgery at the age of 79, he told me he was at peace and said, "I have had a good life, and whatever happens, I am in God's hands." He passed on shortly after the surgery. I'm sure he is still creating and moving on in the realms of Spirit.

For many people, there does come a time when, like it or not, you are 65 or 70 and "retired." Now what? You could lose your whole reason for being and say, My life is over. Or you could say, What's next? What does my Creator have in mind for me now? What do I still want to accomplish in my life? How can I make it happen? What do I need to do to set the stage? With a positive attitude like that, you magnetize new opportunity.

I think of Grandma Moses, who began her painting career in her 80s, Elizabeth Caspari, who at 100 is still visiting the classroom, giving private lessons and being an inspiration to aspiring Montessori teachers, and Mother Teresa, who was still going strong when she passed on in her 80s.

Astronaut John Glenn in his 70s is an example to young and old, as is 80-year-old Pope John Paul. There are many unsung heroes and heroines who have kept on moving and accomplishing after retirement age.

Transforming Our Soul's Sense of Loss into New Beginnings and a Sense of Renewal

Take a moment to go back in memory to a scene of personal loss that you know needs to be healed within yourself. How old are you? What is happening? What are you feeling? What do you think might help you feel better? Accept your intuitive answers, whatever they are.

Now commune with your Higher Self and your soul at the age you were when you experienced that loss. Focus on the vulnerable feelings of this younger part of you that remembers the past with a sense of hurt or frustration. Maybe it's fear, helplessness, worthlessness or hopelessness. Perhaps it's anger, grief or loneliness.

Jot a note to yourself about these feelings. Remember how you felt toward others who were a part of that experience. If you get upset when you remember the situation, you are still carrying those feelings as an inner burden.

Now that you are in touch with your feelings, visualize sharing them with someone you love. You might like to do this in the secret chamber of your heart. Where is that? It is an inner chamber beyond our normal vision of time and space as we know it. Saint Teresa of Àvila called it her "interior castle." It is a special place where we may communicate with God through our Higher Self.

Everyone's secret chamber may be a little different. I see mine as bathed in beautiful golden pink, shimmering light. There is an altar with a flame burning brightly—pink, gold and blue in color. Outside the secret chamber is my own secret garden with all kinds of flowers, shrubs, trees and bluebirds. And beyond my secret garden is a pathway that leads to a beautiful white sandy beach where the ocean waves are gently rolling in. The sun is shining and puffy white clouds float above in the deep blue sky. It is a paradise of beauty and peace.

Take a moment to go within to the secret chamber of your heart. Imagine what this most beautiful and sacred place looks like. It is all your own.

Now imagine walking up a path that leads to the secret chamber of your heart and knocking on the door of that inner chamber. Your Higher Self, Christ Self or Buddha Self welcomes you and bids you enter. Imagine sharing the painful memory with your Inner Teacher in the secret chamber.

Visualize your soul standing before you as the child or person you were at the time of the experience you are remembering. Ask your soul, "What may I do for you right now? I want to understand more about what you are feeling about this loss. I love you, and I want to help you."

As you imagine your soul responding to you, let your soul know that you understand, that you love your soul as every inner part of you—the child, the youth, the adolescent, young adult, middle-age or older person that you are inside. Perhaps you may even contact an ancient embodiment of your soul. Whatever comes, allow it.

If your soul is in pain, stay with the pain. Love yourself through the pain. Stay with it until she feels comforted and protected.

Put your arms around yourself. Visualize embracing your soul. Comfort and care for her. Finally, from a point of deep listening and caring in your heart, ask your Higher Self, "What is our lesson?"

Listen with your heart until you feel an intuitive understanding of the lesson. Determine to learn it. Remind yourself that your loving Father-Mother and the angels are here to heal, love and embrace you as you allow yourself to feel the grief, sadness, anger, fear or shame—to feel the pain and to say to yourself, simply, "I hurt." You may sense your Father-Mother God responding, "I know you hurt, beloved son, beloved daughter. Remember I love you. I am with you always."

Take a few moments to soothe your soul. "I know you hurt, beloved one, and I love you. I am here with you, and the angels are healing our pain." Allow yourself to feel peace and comfort from your inner experience. When you feel complete, offer a prayer of gratitude and ask your Higher Self to help you create a new beginning.

The Great Challenge: Turning Karmic Losses into Transformational Experiences

In situations of endings, it is a great challenge to open our hearts and minds to the possibility of a loss being karmic or heralding a transformational experience. Yet when we do so, we may claim a miraculous new beginning. If, on the other hand, we close our minds and hearts, we may sit around in a blue funk of depression for a long time—and thereby miss opportunities that are knocking at our door.

How do we take the high road here? First, we allow ourselves to experience our feelings fully so that we may gradually move through the pain. Second, we choose to trust our God, to understand that pain does not mean ultimate disaster. We can allow the pain to open our heart and soul. Third, we choose to let go of our negative conclusions about whatever has happened and to be at peace with ourselves during the healing process. Fourth, we open ourselves to new opportunities, to the possibility that something new and beautiful is being born within us.

Each of these steps is challenging at first. A sense of peaceful acceptance in the face of calamity doesn't just come floating out of the ethers. We have to make the choice not to allow this difficult experience to take us away from the plumb line of our inner truth, our integrity, and our relationship with God and the angels. Our relationship with the divine is an inner treasure that no one but ourselves can take from us.

In my studies of the karmic workings of the universe, I have realized that everything that happens to us is likely to be both a karmic lesson and a transformational opportunity. We may think of our relationships and possessions as good and not-so-good karma and our dissolutions and losses as a form of karma balancing. In a cosmic sense, I see everything that we have as God's energy, which the universe kindly allows us to use as our own. When we see it this way, we find ourselves being grateful for what we do have instead of mourning what we don't have or what we have lost.

Last year, in the wake of the Oklahoma tornadoes, I watched a televised scene of a couple who had lost everything—their house and possessions were in splinters and they had no resources. Yet the man was saying, "We still have each other. That's what really matters. We are grateful to be alive, and we'll find a way to make it."

Courage and the can-do spirit—that couple had it. They were accepting their losses and preparing to move on. While we may or may not have a loving earthly mother or father or spouse to reassure us, we always have our connection with God through our Higher Self and the angels. When we ask for help from higher realms, we come to understand life's lessons, to envision new opportunities, and to claim the inner strength to move on.

When we address endings and beginnings in our lives, we are doing healing work with our soul. Our soul is our inner child, our inner adolescent, our inner young adult, our inner middle-age or golden-age person, as well as our ancient soul that has inscribed upon her all the happenings that have led us to the present moment. We heal our soul as we open our heart and mind to the guidance of Spirit and love ourselves through the process of learning, growing and becoming a stronger, wiser and more loving person.

As we encounter the many endings and beginnings of life, we may learn to say a gentle goodbye to the ending and a cheery hello to the new beginning. We may move forward with an enriched knowing of ourselves, our beliefs, our hopes and dreams.

We are like the butterfly coming out of the cocoon. We emerge. We stretch our wings and fly into the sunlight.

Exercise in Endings and Beginnings

1. *Focus on one particular ending that has been difficult for you. Take a moment to go within, to pray, to ask for the assistance of the angels and your Higher Self to help you to move through the hurt feelings, the difficulty of letting go, the sense of loss, the fear or hesitancy to move on.*

2. *Ask for the love, understanding and strength to accept change, to open your eyes, to face the new day, to embrace a new beginning and to do what it takes to make it happen.*

3. *Take a few minutes to meditate, to ask your heart for guidance, and to make a note to yourself about your thoughts, feelings and inner sense of direction.*

4. *Visualize yourself offering forgiveness to those who may have been the instruments of your pain or loss. Ask God to forgive you, and forgive yourself for any mistakes you may have made.*

5. *Thank the angels for that greatest gift of all—the divine love that is anchored in your heart. And give yourself a hug.*

CHAPTER NINE

Cycles of Change: Beyond the Comfort Zone

On the wings of Time,
grief flies away.

—JEAN DE LA FONTAINE

*I*n the turmoil that accompanies cycles of change, most of us feel emotionally uprooted. We face the challenge of how to handle loss, work through grief and move toward renewal when we feel pushed beyond our comfort zone by life itself.

The process of renewal compels us to reach beyond our normal limits, to change our approach to life and often our lifestyle as well. Meanwhile, the winds of change rock the boat of our emotional balance and begin to impact the comfortability of our relationships.

Uncertainty becomes the name of the game. We feel thrust into a mad whirl of only slightly understandable circumstances. In the midst of all this we are expected to maintain a positive attitude, pursue new goals, master new skills and keep our composure. Is it any wonder that people in the throes of change do not necessarily walk around with smiles on their faces? In fact, this experience lends new meaning to the White Rabbit's lament in *Alice in Wonderland* as he hurries along, "I'm late, I'm late, for a very important date...."

Another way most of us relate to the ever-speeding-up pressure to change is that we tend to retreat into ourselves. Sometimes this is healthy strategic withdrawal or a much-needed inner R & R. At other times it is a frantic attempt to escape the complex demands of our new reality by revolving the way it used to be in our minds, which doesn't do us any good. When we try to hold onto the shifting sands of the past, the grains of sand slip through our fingers and we are left with little but a sinking feeling in the pit of our stomach.

When Mr. Change comes to dinner as an invited or uninvited guest, why not welcome him? Invite him in, treat him with respect, and see if we can figure out what he's up to. Of course, it takes a bit of change in our own perspective to do that. A sense of humor helps.

We discover he's not as unpleasant as we thought he might be. In fact, he's rather an interesting fellow. Just as we are beginning to get comfortable with him, the doorbell rings and in hurries his cousin, Miss Frantic Change. She seems a little out of balance, but we determine to be pleasant about it. By the end of the dinner, we have gotten to know them both fairly well. We may even decide to ask them what they can offer to us. At this point we have made the unknown known and are no longer so uptight. Who knows? If we get to know them better, we might learn something.

We might decide to discuss with Mr. and Miss Change how people today feel a loss of stability at work and at home and are often in distress about their financial circumstances and personal relationships. These are real-life dilemmas. Perhaps as we get to know each other better, we can generate a more creative approach. After all, that's what chaos theory tells us. Creativity is all about the creative burst that comes forth from the intersection and interaction of matter and energy. The Change family knows more about the energy part of it. We know more about the matter side. Let's put our heads together on some of the major issues facing us today.

Moving Beyond Divorce And the Grief for What Might Have Been

Let's look at the issue of divorce. Divorce creates grief in the hearts of those who have lost someone who was once dear to them. Usually even the person who is choosing to leave the relationship feels a sense of grief for what might have been.

For the one being left, it's like a slap in the face, figuratively speaking, to see the one you love turning their back on you. It hurts. How do we get through it? It's a process. We ask our Higher Self to help us. We open ourselves to our feelings and allow ourselves to cry, to grieve, until the well of our tears runs dry. As we express and process our feelings, we begin the process of letting go. We are readying ourselves to move toward envisioning and embracing a new beginning.

I remember Joe and Alice—"Such a lovely couple," everyone said when they were first married. Five years later Alice was in my office trying to pick up the pieces of her life after their divorce.

"I kept trying to hang in there," she said, as tears

streamed down her face. "But I couldn't take the abuse. When we were married, he promised to give up the booze. And he did for awhile. But when he got under pressure on the job, he started drinking again. And then he'd take his frustrations out on me. He's like a different person when he's drinking. He's not the man I loved and married."

Alice went on to tell me that after almost five years of frequent abuse, she was the one who finally filed for divorce. She had kept hoping he would change. He refused to go to AA even though he had a friend who went regularly. He said, "I don't need to go listen to a bunch of drunks. I'm not an alcoholic. I just drink too much sometimes. I can stop anytime I really want to."

To prove it, he stayed dry for a few months. Then it began all over again, along with the abuse. When she told Joe she had had enough and was filing for divorce, he finally agreed to try a treatment program. Halfway through, he quit.

At that point Alice knew she was either in for a lifetime of abuse or she had to get out. Fortunately, she chose to get out. She told me that several months after their divorce, Joe was jailed for beating up a girlfriend so badly that she was hospitalized.

"That could have been me," she sobbed. "What happened to the Joe I loved and married? I still love him, I mean the Joe he really is, not the drunk who beat me up over the last five years. Do you think I should have tried harder?"

I reassured Alice that she had done what she had to do, and until Joe himself would decide he wanted to give up drinking, there was little or nothing that anyone else could do for him, even treatment centers. Indeed it could have been Alice in the hospital. Sadly, Alice had little choice but to take her stand and move on.

Through her therapy sessions, Alice began to understand her own codependency, her propensity to try to rescue Joe from himself, and why it didn't work.

She picked up the pieces of her life and moved on, hoping for a better relationship now that she understood herself better. One of the last remarks she made as she left my office after her final session was encouraging.

She said, "I have learned a big lesson. I am going to be on the lookout for that "rescuer" part of me. I am still sad about what happened to Joe and our marriage, but I understand it's not anything I can change. Alcohol is really a beast, but Joe has to live his own life and make his own decisions. All I can do is pray for him and go on with my life. I am going to wait awhile, though, before I get into another relationship."

Alice wrote me several years later to tell me she was remarried to a wonderful man who is a loving husband—and doesn't drink. She wrote, "I still think about Joe sometimes and hope he has stopped drinking. Jim is much more mature than Joe ever was, and he is such a sweet husband and father. We have a little girl, Sandy, and another on the way. I thought you might like to hear about my happy ending!"

I wrote back how happy I was for her. She is a sweet, brave woman who learned a very hard lesson about what alcohol can do to a loved one and to a marriage. She had the courage to be true to herself, to separate out and move on to what became a happy new beginning.

Shedding the Snakeskin of Grief and Sadness

We may discover layers and layers of grief when we are dealing with loss and moving on. Yet each time we allow ourselves to feel it, to learn from it, it's like shedding an old snakeskin. I remember my spiritual teacher saying to me once, "Just step out of that, Marilyn, step out of it!" And I thought to myself, "Step out of what?" After awhile I realized what the "what" was. It was an old mold of gloomy thoughts, sad feelings and habitual ways of reacting to try to avoid getting hurt.

And this is true for all of us. In an energy sense, we can simply step out of it—the sad vibration, the old mode of thinking, the feelings attached to something or someone we have lost, memories and habits formed long ago that no longer serve us. We can step out of all of this. And move on.

Painful Experiences of Loss Offer Special Gifts

Painful experiences of loss offer us special gifts: a deeper understanding of our soul and our purpose in life, the breaking open of our heart, the awakening of compassion, the mobilizing of courage. I have seen these gifts many times in my own life and the lives of my clients. I have come to believe that many of us learn our greatest lessons of love through experiences of loss.

We feel the deep hurt of loss when someone dear to us moves on and we are alone and unsure of what to do next. It is at these very moments that the tender hand of God may touch us because we are hurting, no longer captive to the habitual rhythms of our life and therefore more receptive to inner experience and divine guidance.

I remember a lovely young woman, Sylvia, who lost her father in a serious car accident. She particularly felt the loss because she had lost her mother as a child and her dad had always been there for her when she needed him. She came to me in deep mourning, very frightened and unsure of herself.

She told me, "I feel all alone in the world. I don't know what to do next. I am still upset with the driver of that car that killed my dad, even though I know it was one of those accidents that couldn't be helped. The roads were next to impossible that night. They closed them after the accident.

"I have asked God to help me forgive the man. Lord knows he feels terrible enough. He came to see me to tell me how sorry he was and to ask if he could do anything for me. He's an older man, like my dad. All I could think of was, my dad would know what to do. Isn't that ridiculous?"

I understood how she felt. She actually appreciated the kindness of the man who had been driving the other car, yet she was torn with feelings of helplessness, pain and sorrow. She was used to turning to her father when life was tough, and he was no longer there.

I remember comforting her and asking if she had ever

had to face something this difficult before without her father's help.

"No," she said. "That's the trouble. I guess I always expected Dad to pick up the pieces whenever I needed him. He always did. Now I find myself almost resenting that he didn't teach me how—and yet he did, by example. Oh, I don't know. I'm all mixed up."

I assured her that it was natural to be all mixed up right now. After several sessions where we focused on her grief and sense of helplessness, she looked at me and said, "You know, my dad actually did teach me by his example. I think he would expect me to pick up the pieces myself, and he'd probably be kind of proud of me if I did."

I agreed. "It sounds like your dad was a pretty great guy. He's probably looking down at you right now, wishing he could help and cheering you on."

Sylvia smiled, "That would be like him. Maybe that's what I could do next—remember what he would do if he were here helping me pick up the pieces and try to do it for myself. But it's still scary."

I certainly understood that. "Sylvia, of course it's scary, but with your dad rooting for you, I bet you can do it. How can I help you?"

She responded, "Maybe you could help me come up with a plan to move forward. Dad always said I had a good head on my shoulders when I put it on." She laughed a little as she added, "I guess I'm about to put it on."

We worked out a plan together for her to go on with

her life, step-by-step. My admiration and respect for this young woman grew weekly as I watched her think each step through, deal with her fear and step forward anyway. She discovered she wasn't as helpless as she thought.

The crowning moment came when she laughingly said to me, "Well, my dad can applaud himself and me. He did a really good job of being the example, and I'm doing a really good job of becoming everything he taught me."

I couldn't have said it better myself. I replied, "I can't think of a higher tribute you could give to your dad than putting on his best qualities and joining them with your own. And I am sure that wherever he is, he is applauding and cheering you on."

It wasn't all roses, of course, and Sylvia still had her ups and downs as she continued to work her way through grief, apprehension and a few false starts. Sometimes the panic would return briefly, and then she would get a grip again.

There were moments of awakening when she felt the intercession of the angels and her Higher Self, whom she knows as her Christ Self. I credit a lot of Sylvia's progress to the fact that she talked to the angels and asked them to help her every day and that she had a relationship with her God through her Higher Self. Each session we would pray for God, the angels and her Christ Self to guide us.

As Sylvia continued to process her feelings, she began to have a vision of her new direction and how to make it happen. As she followed through on her plans, her hopelessness, helplessness and sense of powerlessness gradually disappeared—replaced by renewed hope and a new beginning.

Overall, Sylvia claimed her new beginning in a most magnificent way—facing her feelings squarely, going through the process of forgiveness, standing on her own two feet even when almost overwhelmed with fear, and choosing to get on with life without dad. I have always remembered her because she was a person who chose to turn disaster into opportunity. She took courage to forge a new direction and moved on with her life.

Sylvia called me several years later to let me know she was getting married. I was very happy for her and told her I knew her father and mother would be, too.

She said, "Yes, I think so, too. I'm kind of proud of myself, in a good way. I want you to know that I'm marrying a man who really appreciates my "get up and go." I'm so glad I picked up the pieces and went on. I can scarcely relate to the scared rabbit I was when I first came in to see you after the accident. Of course, I still miss my dad. But I have this very strong sense of becoming much more of who I really am through all of this. Maybe that was part of God's plan for me."

I couldn't have agreed more. I breathed a prayer of gratitude and blessing for this lovely soul and for the happiness of her oncoming marriage.

Exercise: Expanding Your Comfort Zone

1. *Take several deep breaths, exhaling slowly. Focus your attention on your breathing and the gentle beating of your heart and enjoy the relaxed feeling.*

2. *Remember a time when you felt peaceful, comfortable, content. Stay with those good feelings for a few minutes.*

3. *Now imagine an experience that would propel you beyond your comfort zone. Notice what you are thinking and feeling. Be aware of any physical sensations.*

4. *Ask your Higher Self, What is God trying to teach me here? Meditate on it until you understand the lesson.*

5. *Send love and gratitude to your Higher Self for giving you understanding, and imagine yourself handling the experience in a positive way.*

6. *Practice, privately, doing what you have imagined until you are comfortable with it. Now give yourself a pat on the back for expanding your comfort zone.*

CHAPTER TEN

Transformational Stages of Grief and Renewal

Make me to say,
when all my griefs are gone,
Happy the heart that sighed
for such a one!
—Samuel Daniel

*P*rofessionals have a lot of different ways of looking at the dimensions of grief, but we all agree on some of the basics. Let us look at the various stages of grief that most people experience after a major loss, starting with *shock and denial.*

Shock and Denial

Our first reaction to any kind of loss is a sense of shock, numbness and a sense of disbelief. We say, "No! I can't believe it. This can't be happening." We remain in a state of shock anywhere from a few hours to a few days or many weeks. Some people move on naturally, while others seem frozen in place and need help.

Have you known someone who has experienced a great loss, such as the loss of a loved one, a job shift or a major financial setback, who seemed to march on with great stoicism? Perhaps this person made a quick recovery, but more likely he or she was still in shock.

I have seen people at funerals or memorial services who were gracious, charming and seemingly in perfect control of themselves. The reality was that the loss hadn't really registered yet. They were in a state of shock and didn't realize it.

Everyone is in shock at first. It's like a temporary anesthesia. Perhaps it's God's way and nature's way of softening the blow by letting us temporarily escape from the painful reality. It helps us along until we are ready to feel the depth of the loss. Some people just keep busy with their usual activities until it finally hits home.

It is helpful to have someone near by to give us loving support, but it's also important to do whatever we can for ourselves. Our normal routines of self-care remind us that we are alive and well, and caring for ourselves helps us move through shock or denial. Once we accept the reality of the loss and our feelings about it, we begin a healing process.

Anger

Sometimes we become angry. We feel like shouting to the universe, "Why did this have to happen?" The intensity of the anger reveals the depth of pain. We may blame ourselves or someone else for our misery. We may even try to blame God: "Why did you do this to me?"

Anger is a step on this journey of transformation as we try to mobilize strength. Underneath the anger lies the hurt, and we need a healthy release for our feelings. Physical exercise is a good release, especially swimming. Being submerged in a pool of water is very nurturing to the body—and to the soul.

Some people find screaming a great release, but I don't. Screaming sets up highly energized vibrations that can be harmful and frightening to others. The vibration goes out all over the universe. Even in an enclosed room, screaming one's anger can cause problems because the vibration remains active for a long time.

Others write a letter to the person they are angry with—and burn it. Putting one's thoughts on paper discharges the anger in a harmless way. A very positive way of releasing feelings and body tensions is to play a favorite musical instrument, sing to one's self or listen to uplifting music. Remember, it is music that "soothes the savage beast."

A spiritual practice that has helped many of my clients is the "Buddha under the Bodhi Tree" exercise at the end of chapter 4. In this case, we pick our favorite spot for meditation, sit quietly and allow feelings of anger to come up while we simply observe them. We acknowledge and give space to our anger without acting on it, holding on to it, denying it or pushing it away. As we observe the anger with nonattachment, the feelings move and change. In the ebb and flow of mixed feelings, we contact the underlying pain.

Pain

We touch the depths of our pain. It hurts. We allow ourselves emotional release. Sometimes tears well up in spite of our best efforts to control them. Allow them. Tears are nature's gentle way of releasing pain.

We cry. The wellspring of our pain is released through the blessed relief of tears. Tears are a gift from God; they express what words cannot say. Tears open us to the pain and the core of our soul; they reveal our feelings, our vulnerability, our tenderness. Even though we may feel alone while crying, tears connect us with each other, with God, with all humanity through this powerful energy being released.

So we let go and cry and eventually give ourselves a comforting hug. If we have someone close to us who can give us a hug, that's great, too. We need to express the emotions we are feeling, and it's a great comfort when someone who understands responds with loving attention, a warm heart, a friendly hug and a helping hand. It helps to remember that God always understands and we can turn to Him for comfort.

We may bring out remembrances, pictures of our loved one who has gone on, letters, cards, messages from that one over the years. We are somewhat eased by remembering the past. Such quiet contemplation helps us gently move through the pain.

Depression

We may feel bereft, lonely and despondent. It's like the sun isn't shining even though it is. In our depressed world, the clouds cover everything, and we find ourselves feeling gloomy, maybe very gloomy.

Depression is truly a dark night of the soul. It heralds an opportunity to let go of our attachments to the world, to people we love. Within this deeply painful, stripping experience are buried the seeds of new growth.

As we go through this deep soul-searching period, it is like the death of a part of us, a part of our life, even if it is not the death of a loved one. We may envision this part of the grieving process as letting go of whomever or whatever we have lost, and gradually healing the wound.

We allow ourselves to be aware of our hurt, sorrow and loneliness and to begin the painful job of self-reflection, honest evaluation and soul-searching. Although the process is emotionally difficult, we are moving on with our healing. In the midst of depression, it is helpful to remember, "This will not last forever; it is always darkest before the dawn."

One day, no matter how long or short a time before it comes, the dark clouds pass. For life is a series of sine waves, ups and downs, peaks and valleys, and the sun always comes out eventually. In the meantime, we simply determine to keep on moving.

Turning to a comforting, reassuring friend during this time can help a lot. Or we may decide to talk to a counselor or minister. Sometimes the clouds roll away swiftly, and sometimes they take weeks, months or even years.

Everyone has his or her own emotional timetable, so don't ever let anybody tell you that you should be getting over your grief. It isn't up to anyone but you and God to know what your timetable is. If you know you want to move on and still feel stuck, that's when you may benefit from getting some help from a therapist.

Guilt

We may feel a sense of guilt about the loss, as if we have done something wrong. We return to our childlike state where when something bad happened we thought it was our fault.

As children, our perspective revolves very much around ourselves. Only as we mature do we include the reality of another person's part in whatever is happening. When we are suffering from loss, we feel helpless and vulnerable and childlike. We are likely to wonder if we did something to cause the loss, whether we did or not.

I know of very few people who have had a close relative or friend pass on or who have lost their job who do not have at least a twinge of guilt. We torture ourselves with thoughts like, "If I had just done such and such, maybe it would have made a difference. Or maybe if I hadn't done such and such, it wouldn't have happened."

We need to say to ourselves, "Okay, this is normal guilt. But it's not real. I'll take responsibility for what is real, but not for what wasn't my fault. I am going to let go of these guilt feelings. The fact is that this person I lost was on God's timetable." Or if it was the loss of a job, "My job was on God's timetable. The angels will point me to something new just around the corner."

Forgiveness

If we continue to believe that we have done something wrong, we may pray or write a letter to God, admitting our mistake and asking for forgiveness. It is helpful to burn this letter to symbolize that we are surrendering the situation to Him. At the conclusion of this ritual, we accept the return current of God's love, understanding and forgiveness.

Now we try to forgive ourselves, to forgive our human

flaws and our karmic predicament. We admit to ourselves, "I know I have made mistakes. I am sorry, and I will make amends. Even though I made those mistakes, I choose to accept God's forgiveness and to forgive myself. I chose to move on."

If someone has passed on, left us, deserted us or is no longer here for us for whatever reason, we utter a little prayer of forgiveness toward that person so that our soul may feel free to love and to let go. We might write that person a letter letting them know that we love him or her. As we burn the letter, we choose to let go. *To love and to let go* —that is the secret of healing our sense of loss and beginning the gradual process of renewal.

Resistance to Life

Even once we have chosen to love and let go, we may resist returning to our normal life. After a great loss, it's almost too painful to step back into life. Some people become reclusive to the point that they literally make hermits of themselves. Aloneness is good, but not to the point where we shut ourselves off from life.

Life may seem somewhat unreal. We may feel as if we aren't really there even as we go through the process of making the beds, cooking for the family, visiting with friends and going on with our job responsibilities.

This is a natural part of this stage of grief. Part of our resistance to resuming our lifestyle may be some leftover guilt. It's almost as if we believe we do not deserve to go on with our life as though nothing has happened. So we hold ourselves back.

Gradually we overcome our hesitancy. Getting out in nature is often helpful. Putting our attention on our senses helps us feel more alive. We may practice noticing what we see, feel, hear, smell and taste. As we do so, we sharpen our senses to life once again. Nature helps us connect to our inner being.

Our goal is to let go gradually of whatever we are holding onto in the past so that we may embrace the present and welcome the future. We can ask God to help us. Just a simple prayer will do, such as "Dear God, I'm trying to get back into life now. Please help me."

It is also helpful to have friends who encourage us to resume more responsibilities at home, with family, friends, our job or career. Gradually we start living again—living in the sense of taking charge of our life and readying ourselves for a new beginning.

Fear

We often fear coming alive again, being hurt again. We seek the courage to restore our faith in ourselves. We may even need to restore our faith in God, whom we may blame at some level for our loss.

We can become panicky. We tend to get panicky when we are trying to let go or accept the ending of something important to us, especially if a new beginning is not fully in sight. We keep grabbing on to whatever it is we have lost. Then we panic because it isn't there after all. It's gone its way. We realize it's kind of crazy thinking, but we don't know what else to do.

This is simply another aspect of grief. For some people it may last only a few moments. For others, it lasts longer. We might benefit from doing a reality check with friends during this time. Or perhaps a counselor or wise older person can help us put it all back into perspective, to realize that fear is a part of the normal process of grief.

One of the greatest opportunities loss gives us is a chance to face our fears and conquer them. These are easy words but a very difficult task. Yet we are up to it when we ask for help and guidance from upstairs.

Every time we face our fear and claim our courage, we conquer that fear. We expand our heart. Any lesson that comes from claiming our courage is very precious. We learn that the bogeyman of fear is just that—a monster that isn't real. When we mobilize courage, we pass right through our fear.

Hope

We begin to catch a glimpse of light at the end of the tunnel. We dare to hope, to envision the darkness subsiding, the sun rising. Whether it's weeks, months or years, as we allow ourselves to express our thoughts and feelings and to care for ourselves lovingly, we move toward a new beginning.

With our hand in God's hand, hope gradually comes through and we know we are on our way up. And when we put hope together with action, we can make our dream of a positive new beginning come true.

Rebirth

We emerge from our journey through loss and grief. We enter the land of the living. We embrace our new beginning. We affirm the reality of the here and now, "Here I am, my two feet on planet Earth. The sun is shining, or maybe it's not, but whichever it is, here I am. This is what is real, my here and now."

Often a deeper faith in God comes from these experiences of endings and loss. We come to a deeper understanding of the pathos of the human condition. The French have a saying, "The heart must break or turn to stone." Our heart is open because we have allowed it to break open instead of sealing it shut.

The reality of life, according to Buddhic teachings, is that there are ten thousand joys and ten thousand sorrows. And so it is. Life is all about the sine waves, the ups and the downs of energy flow and of cycles of change. Even when our mastery of ourselves increases and we have more ups than downs, we still have occasional down moments. That may not be our favorite thing, but it can be okay.

Thus the Buddha came to his awareness of the necessity for nonattachment and the Eightfold Path of desirelessness because he loved people and wanted to relieve their suffering. When we cultivate loving nonattachment and self-mastery, we ready ourselves for a life of rebirth and renewal.

Transformation

Our heart has broken open. We feel more compassionate, more giving and more alive. We ultimately are richer for our experience. We come to realize that the pain that has broken our heart has also initiated a flow of love, of appreciation of life and opportunity, of a deeper understanding of life and empathy with others.

We have become more of who we really are. We have come to know ourselves as sensitive, courageous people. We who have known the pain of loss and grief may, in turn, help others because we know that beyond the dark clouds is a new horizon. We have been there. We have come out the other side. We become a comforting resource for friends and loved ones.

We find ourselves more appreciative of the rhythm of life and the opportunities we have. We appreciate the *here and now*, the present moment of living. We may be less shy about expressing love and appreciation to others because we have passed through our own deep valley of pain.

Above all, we have deepened our relationship with our God. We have felt the comfort of the angels, of our Higher Self, of masters of love who have brought us through this dark night of the soul. We have more of an appreciation for the light, for opportunity, for the gift of life. We have come to a realization of the cycles of life, that they come and go, here one day, gone the next—yet God is in His heaven and all is right with our world.

Greeting the New Day

We choose to live more fully, to savor every moment of our day, to give more grace to others, to be less moved by trivial disappointments or annoyances, to be more forgiving and understanding. All of these are gifts of the transformational cycle of loss, grief and renewal.

We offer a prayer of thanksgiving for a new opportunity, a new perspective. And we are grateful for the ever-abiding presence of the angels and angel-friends on earth who have seen us through the dark night into the dawn of the new day.

We reclaim our joy. As Kahlil Gibran put it so beautifully, "Your joy is your sorrow unmasked. And the selfsame well from which your laughter rises was oftentimes filled with your tears. And how else can it be? The deeper that sorrow carves into your being, the more joy you can contain."[1]

The Blessing of Renewal

In his lovely book, *Gentle Roads to Survival*, Andrew Auw offers a moving description of his personal experience with the death of his sister, which brought him to a transcendent experience and the blessing of renewal in which he overcame his fear of death.

He writes, "The sudden death of my sister in an automobile accident left me stunned. After the grief, I began to reflect on the brevity of her life and on plans she had made that could not be completed. Then I saw a parallel in my own life. With this awareness I began to focus my energy on living more in the present moment than in the past or the future. I started noticing things: clouds, birds, sunsets, the smell of the sea breeze, the warmth in a glance, the love in a touch. Then a marvelous thing happened: I lost my fear of death. It was as if the more I began to live life, the less reason I had to worry about the last stage of life. My initial loss was extremely painful, but the ensuing gain was a whole new sense of the meaning of life itself."[2]

Meditation: Loving and Letting Go

Here is a meditation for loving and letting go of pain that you can do in your own special place of meditation or prayer, or perhaps inwardly in the secret chamber of your heart:

Visualize the sun rising, the angels surrounding you, flowers in bloom, blue sky, white clouds, your own beautiful secret garden, a sandy beach by the ocean or a glade of ferns and flowers in the forest. Or see yourself standing on a mountaintop viewing the beauty of nature all around you.

Now visualize yourself letting go of the pain, embracing yourself, embracing life and the new day. Imagine turning to your beloved who has gone on and saying goodbye. "I love you and I am saying goodbye for now. I am welcoming the new day. I send you on with my love and blessing."

Visualize angels and heavenly beings welcoming your beloved if he or she has passed on, or guiding that one if he or she has simply moved to a different place in life. Then visualize yourself walking into the sun. Even though tears may continue to fall, through those tears you may see the rainbow of God's love uplifting your heart and soul. Visualize yourself becoming one with that rainbow of eternal promise.

When you have completed your meditation, take a few moments to write a letter, poem or story or draw a picture about the lessons you have learned and the new beginning you glimpse, even if it's not quite there yet. What is the lesson for your soul? It's always a lesson of the heart, one way or another. Ask your heart to help you understand the lesson.

What gift may you take from this experience that you may offer to your soul, to your life and to the lives of others? How may you enrich life with your special gift? How may you bless the earth because you have chosen to move beyond the via dolorosa—the "sorrowful way"? Make some notes to yourself so that you may look back on them later.

Now choose to welcome the new day! Look around you with an eye to seeing the beauty of God's world, the new possibilities for your life, the new friendships you may cultivate, the ongoing ones you may continue to nurture.

CHAPTER ELEVEN

The Gift of Living Fully in the Present

⚜

This is the day which the Lord
hath made; we will rejoice
and be glad in it.
—PSALM 118:24

$\mathcal{E}$ach of us has the opportunity to accept and welcome the gift of living fully in the present. When we awaken to the eternal here and now, we feel alive, mobilized, our senses quickened. Each moment fully experienced becomes an integral part of the sculpting of our future. As we live today, we create our tomorrows.

Today we may choose to be happy, cheerful and kind, to do our creative best at work, to relax in play. We may embrace life, accept and learn from the good and the not-so-good moments, appreciate and understand our family, friends and colleagues and support and forgive one another when difficulties arise.

All of these choices represent a creative way of living the fullness of our day. When we spend a day that way, we feel great when we go to bed. We have done our part to create a happy, productive tomorrow.

By contrast, if we spend the day grumbling, groaning, sad, depressed, resentful, withdrawn, fearful or angry, we're not having a very good today—and we are definitely not creating a good tomorrow.

Think about it. We are offered many choices. We choose how we perceive and handle life's happenings. We choose how we want to respond to each experience in our life. With every choice we carve another aspect of our future.

Pain as an Essential Inner Teacher

We can actually reach a point where a sudden happening and the accompanying loss or pain is not such a big deal. We accept that pain is simply a part of life. We cut our finger, and it heals. We lose friends and gain new ones. We smart from the hurt of someone's unkind action and either work it out with that person or decide to let it go. Wounds, losses, pain—yes, they do hurt, but pain itself is a part of the healing process.

Think of people who are born without pain receptors, who do not feel pain. They often injure their bodies terribly. They can put their hand on a hot stove and not feel it and come away with the tissue totally burned. So pain is a teacher; pain is a warning; pain is a signal. It's a type of inner radar that says, "Hey, there's something happening you need to pay attention to."

As the Tibetan Master, Djwal Kul, once said, "Pain has no dominion over you, but pain is an essential teacher.... Embrace her, move through her, beyond her and find your manifest reality."[1]

When we are faced with pain, we may choose to explore it, to understand it and to learn the soul lesson inherent in it. The secret is keeping our heart open. Think of the avatars and the saints. They kept their hearts open even when they suffered great pain. Jesus and Gautama kept their hearts open. Padre Pio, Mahatma Gandhi and Mother Teresa kept their hearts open. We may choose to walk in their footsteps.

As we allow ourselves to realize we are wounded, to be aware of the pain and go deeper and deeper to its source, we reach deep into the well of our being to release old hurts, old poisons. That's why we embrace pain. It's not because we love the fact that it hurts. Nobody likes to hurt. But we choose to embrace pain because it's a piercing, an opening of a wound that allows the hurtful poison to be released. Then we can let it heal.

Think about that for a minute. Isn't it true that we tend to hold on to what we have? Even if it's poisonous, at least it's familiar. So we hold on to old wounds, old ideas, old grudges by thinking about them, recreating them. Whether it is a person, a lifestyle, family, friends or simply our way of doing things—whatever we hold on to gives us pain when it goes its way. When we release our attachment, we feel surcease from the pain.

Be Awake! with the Nonattachment of Buddha

The Buddha as the Enlightened One taught nonattachment because he understood this process. How did he get there? Through communion with God and his determination to be awake. The Buddha said we all need to be *awake!* We need to be awake to greet the new day—with new eyes, new perspective, new hopes and dreams.

We deny ourselves this awakened state when we stay stuck in our pain. Our awareness doesn't extend beyond the pain and the fixed ideas we may have about what is causing it. Or it may be that we try to hide from our feelings, from fully experiencing the pain. When we do this, we feel upset, tense, boxed in. Yet it is a box of our own making.

It's as if we are holding tightly to the past with our eyes firmly shut to the present. Of course, with closed eyes, we can't see the new day, the new opportunity, the possibility of a lesson learned, a gain of new perspective. What to do? We may choose to open our eyes, even as we open our hearts and turn on the awareness of our five outer senses and our sixth sense—our intuition.

What is intuition anyway? It's that sense of inner knowing that comes from being "awake." Buddha's state of awakeness is not as far from our grasp as we might think. It is the awakening of our soul to inner perceptions, inner truths, inner wisdom. You have probably experienced this state many times in your life without even realizing it. It's a part of our spiritual nature that we sometimes take for granted. Life sure is a lot easier when we allow our intuition to guide us.

Of course, this doesn't mean that difficult life situations are always going to "come up roses." But every time we meditate, pray, contemplate and take positive action, we learn and grow. Our victories strengthen our faith, and defeats bring lessons our souls need to learn.

Either way, when we choose to be awake, aware and grateful in the present moment, we offer ourselves the best opportunity for happiness today. In so doing, we create a better tomorrow. And you know what? We may catch a glimpse of the angels smiling.

Humor Helps in the Ups and Downs of Life

Our sense of happiness also has to do with the way we choose to look at misfortune. We may look only at the downside or we may choose to discover an upside. The choice is up to us.

Do you remember the folktale of the old man whose only horse disappeared? When his friends tried to console him, the old man said, "How do you know this isn't a lucky omen?"

Sure enough, after several months, the lost horse came back home accompanied by another excellent horse. Now he had two fine steeds. When the old man's friends congratulated him on his good luck, he replied, "How do you know that's not a bad omen?"

Sure enough! One day the old man's son fell off the horse and broke his leg severely. It left him crippled. When the old man's friends called to tell him how sorry they were, he responded, "How do you know this isn't a good omen?"

As the story goes, shortly after the man's son broke his leg, all the young men in the land were ordered into the army to fight a war far away. However, the old man's son, lame from his accident, was spared.

We could carry this story on and on. It illustrates the ups and downs of life, which we may view as misfortune or opportunity, depending on the way we look at them. Sometimes the seemingly tragic or insolvable dilemma of today is only a prelude to a great opportunity of tomorrow—especially when we choose to look at it that way.

When we accept the misfortunes of today as a potential blessing for tomorrow, we put in motion positive energy that helps make it happen. It's like noticing the silver lining of the clouds—when the clouds move on, we discover the sun has been shining brightly all the time. In our inner world, we begin to move the storm clouds along by focusing on loving, creative thoughts and feelings.

Another way of nurturing a hopeful attitude in the present is to keep your sense of humor alive and well. A good laugh relaxes our body and mind even as it lifts our spirits. A sense of humor about the slightly ridiculous aspects of life generates laughter, and the joyful energy of laughter brings a brighter perspective.

When we stay in the here and now of the present, we find more laughter and fewer tears. The problem for many of us is that we bury the tears of yesterday and carry them into our tomorrows. Instead, let's choose to cry when we are hurt, smile when we are happy and welcome each new day with hope and humor.

Now you might be thinking, "I don't usually wake up feeling hopeful and humorous. In fact, until I get my first cup of coffee, it's better if I don't talk to anybody." Let's take a look at this: You could moan and groan all day—especially if you discover you are out of coffee.

Or you could see the funny side of the drama: "Hmmm, here I am basing my whole day on passing feelings and a cup of coffee. That's pretty ridiculous!" Cartoonists are masters at taking the minor mishaps of our lives and satirically showing us the humor of our ways.

What does it take to cultivate a sense of humor about our mishaps? Perspective. Adopting an attitude of positive expectancy instead of gloom and negative pronouncements.

I remember a friend who had limited finances. When she was in dire need, she would always say, "I'm expecting a check." One time I asked her, "Who from?" She said, "I don't know, but I'm expecting a check."

The delightful truth of this story is that this woman would suddenly get checks out of nowhere. Money seemed to drop from the skies in envelopes addressed to Ruth Farnam. It was as if once she set her consciousness with positive expectation and perfect faith, the universe complied.

Planting Seeds of Love and Hope for Our Future

People have written and talked about this phenomenon as having a "positive mental attitude."[2] I believe it is a natural law of the universe that whatever we send out to life returns to us. We know this from our interactions with people every day. When our heart is full of love, everything seems to move along harmoniously. When we put out negative vibes and verbiage, we get it right back. We would do well to follow Thumper's advice in the movie, *Bambi:* "If you can't say somethin' nice, don't say nuthin' at all!"[3] The lesson here: Whatever we send out, we get back. Karma is our teacher!

Each of us puts on many faces, sometimes all in the course of a day. We take on different outlooks depending on our circumstances, companions, thoughts and desires. As Piero Ferucci puts it, "Life may appear to us at any time as a routine, a dance, a race, an adventure, a nightmare, a riddle, a merry-go-round, etc."[4]

In a word, we have the opportunity to see life as a cup half-full or a cup half-empty. When we see our cup of life half-empty and draining, we feel drained and empty. When we see our cup of life half-full and filling, we feel energized and overflowing. It is all a matter of the perspective we choose.

What Is My Gift to the Earth?
What Can I Do to Bless Someone Today?

So now what? We have picked up the pieces of our broken heart and "put them back together again." We have a renewed sense of direction for our lives and are ready to move forward. Now we arrive at the necessity of will and determination.

How have great artists, musicians, poets, artisans, statesmen, scientists, writers produced finished works? First they experienced a moment of vision or inspiration that filled them with inner illumination. They forged that inner "knowing" into tangible works through a mighty thrust of will, determination and physical effort. The process of bringing their inner vision into physical form took dedication, perseverance and minute-to-minute attention to detail.

Every creative venture has its moments when it would be easy to say, "This is too much, it's hopeless." The person with will and determination says, "This is challenging, and I will find a way to make it work." The first person is saying, "I give up;" the second, "I will make it happen." Who do you think is going to win a victory over challenging circumstances?

Think of Noah building the ark. All those years people made fun of him, yet he maintained his communion with his God and kept on building. He had a strong will, determination and a vision to fulfill. A divine mandate from God. What if Noah had sat down and said to himself, "This is impossible. Forget it!" God could not have continued to work through him because he would no longer have been the chalice of vision, determination, effort and will to accomplish God's work.

Throughout the ages, saints, heroes and heroines inspired to follow a higher vision have mobilized the will, determination and effort to bring that vision to fruition. Think of Joan of Arc, known as the saviouress of France. She had her vision, her "voices" and her dedication to God and country—the France she loved so dearly. Even as she earnestly pursued her destiny, she was known for her sense of humor and laughter.

Joan gave her life for her country, and she is remembered and honored today for her vision, courage and fiery determination to fulfill her mission. One young girl who followed God's direction and took action in the present became the impetus to the future of France as a free country.

Great men and women throughout history have followed their inner vision and sense of destiny to produce heroic and memorable deeds that have changed the course of history. Madame Curie, Clara Barton, Albert Einstein, Louis Pasteur, Jonas Salk and scores of others less well known have dedicated their lives to discoveries that have blessed the lives of people everywhere.

Life on planet Earth is transformed moment to moment by the choices we make and the actions we take. Let's ask ourselves, "What is my gift to the earth? What may I do to bless someone today? How can I help make this world a better place?"

Exercise: Applying History's Ennobling Lessons of Courage and Honor

1. *How can you apply history's lessons of courage in your life today?*

2. *How can you apply history's lessons of honor in your life today?*

3. *What other qualities of heroes or heroines would help you to forge a victorious path homeward?*

4. *How do you think your life might change for the better if you choose to act courageously no matter how scared you feel?*

5. *How do you think your life might change for the better if you choose to uphold the code of honor in your thoughts, words and deeds?*

CHAPTER TWELVE

The Alchemy of Self-Transcendence

To every thing there is a season,
and a time to every purpose
under the heaven.
—ECCLESIASTES 2:16

*W*e have been feeling the rippling of the waves of Aquarius for the past ten to twenty years—and now they are upon us. Which way will civilization go in this new millennium? Will we spiral downward into mass hatred, war, fear, restriction and bondage? Or will we as citizens of planet Earth bring forth an age of love, creativity, innovation and freedom?

Which is it going to be? The answer depends upon each of us and how we choose to live our lives. Will we choose fear and hatred? Or will we choose love and compassion?

The Phoenix Bird Rises from the Ashes

When there is chaos, destruction or personal pain and loss, there is always the promise of rebirth and regeneration because it is the nature of God. No matter how seemingly hopeless the circumstance, the essence of life is to regenerate. Come what may, chaos will redefine itself as natural order reemerges.

Thus, even in the midst of seeming devastation, the phoenix bird rises out of the ashes as the very essence of life seeks renewal. For us as souls walking the earth, we seek that renewal through connectedness with one another and expressing our soul's raison d'être. Thus we find fulfillment in helping one another, building community, creating a new world. Perhaps the true giving nature of the heart is our most precious asset.

Isn't this the quintessence of rebirth, not only for ourselves but also for our culture—allowing love to nurture the soul and to transform our everyday world? No matter how close we get to rock bottom, when we tap into the wellspring of goodwill and compassion of the heart, the regenerating spiral begins.

The Choice for True Freedom: The Freedom to Be All of Who We Really Are

True freedom means to me the freedom for each one of us to become our highest and best self, to reach for the stars, to walk the earth as creative, compassionate explorers, offering our gifts and talents to those we meet along the way.

How we choose to live our lives and who we become is up to each one of us. Have you thought deeply about what freedom means to you? If not, you might take some time to do it now. Does freedom mean high adventure? No, not necessarily. Does it mean freedom from responsibility? Actually, it's just the opposite. Does it mean doing exactly what you please? Not at all.

Freedom is the opportunity to *be*—to be who you really are, to live what you believe, to relate to others with honor and integrity. It means to dream your dreams and make them happen, to bless people you meet by loving them for who they are, to honor your God and the spark of the divine in yourself and others. These are the elements of freedom. True freedom comes from an awakened heart that honors information and innovation as stepping-stones to life-enriching discoveries for the blessing of humanity.

As the earth enters the age of Aquarius, we are meant to become adepts of love and freedom. Whatever our outer appearance, the mystical spark of our divine identity is nurtured in the secret chamber of our heart. In this inner sanctuary burns a sacred flame of divine power, wisdom and love that ancient masters and modern-day mystics refer to as "the threefold flame of life."[1]

Every interaction in life becomes an opportunity to expand that sacred flame of our inner being. Ultimately, our souls, in concert with sacred vision, creative thinking, benevolent feelings and illumined action, are liberated from the bondage of our pseudo-self.

As adepts, we are meant to discern accurately what is going on and to take action accordingly. Sometimes we need to take a firm stand and at other times to gentle our approach with love. You might say that sometimes we need to step on the gas, at other times to lube the gears, and we always need the wisdom of the heart in the driver's seat.

It's a Matter of Intention and Balance

People ask me how they can express empowerment without becoming overbearing or tough. It's a matter of intention and balance. We may determine to claim empowerment as inner strength at the same time that we relate to others with compassionate understanding.

Sometimes people realize the importance of the heart's

insight and understanding in resolving difficult life happenings, yet they do not know how to outwit entrenched mental habits that get in the way. Again, it is a matter of intention and balance. We can determine to listen to our intuition, the prompting of the heart, and then think of a creative way of responding rather than allowing a habitual mind-set to run the show. This can become a daily practice.

Everybody secretly desires love, but many people ask me how to avoid the entrapments that seem to come along with it. It's still a matter of intention and balance. When we express love as compassion balanced with wisdom and inner empowerment, we stay out of the entrapments of sympathy, co-dependence and self-pity. We fulfill our soul's intention to pursue our inner destiny of oneness with Divine Love, which is the true essence of the Father-Mother God. Thus, we set the stage for our return home to God and reunion with our twin soul.[2]

Our Life Is a Sacred Adventure

Many people today are in tune with their mission as they have been listening to their soul and Higher Self and walking a spiritual path. They think of their journey through life as a sacred adventure. They seek to fulfill the destiny of their soul, and they are searching for down-to-earth ways to do it.

For those who are beginning to explore their soul's sense of destiny and specific mission in this life, Laurie Beth Jones' creative book *The Path* provides inspiring and practical advice. With humor and practicality, Laurie Beth offers a step-by-step guide to defining and fulfilling one's mission—including how to create a mission statement and many practical "how-tos."[3]

Once we have defined our mission, we outline a process by which we move steadily toward what we want to accomplish. This is where our will and determination, discussed earlier, becomes all-important. Each day we set our sail of purpose toward the next horizon, leaving room for change due to shifting tides of circumstance or unstable human climate. Our compass is set by our inner sense of destiny and our rudder held steady by the principles and values we hold dear.

Thomas à Kempis gives relevant and practical advice in *The Imitation of Christ*. He says, "In the morning fix thy good purpose; and at eventide examine thy ways, how thou hast behaved thyself this day in word, deed, and thought."[4]

This is excellent counsel to keep ourselves on track as we seek to fulfill our mission. When we stay our mind and heart on God and examine our heart and soul, we draw ever closer to our sense of the sacred. We feel the Presence of God guiding us through our Higher Self—as an inner prompting, an intuitive knowing, a gentle push in the right direction.

We do ourselves a great favor when we take the time to examine our progress on a daily basis. Our divine purpose becomes increasingly clear as we continue to go within and strengthen our partnership with our Higher Self.

We make our mission come alive by envisioning what our life will look like once we complete it. We may want to create a treasure map as a focus for our spiritual alchemy and to keep our consciousness on course. A treasure map is a sort of poster on which we put pictures of who we want to become and things we would like to acquire or accomplish. It serves to "map" a visualization of our future.

We remind ourselves daily of the higher values and principles that we have chosen to live by. We set goals and timelines in order to move forward. Even as we set up an overall strategy to accomplish particular goals, we maintain flexibility and openness to creative ideas and innovative methods that emerge along the way. Remember that chaos, metamorphosis and change are expected and are part of the transformational process.

We open ourselves first to the genius of our Higher Self and then to the experts and innovators of our times. In so doing, we often come up with intuitive ways of approaching and resolving problems that go beyond our original matrix. That's progress!

Many solutions and inventions have come to their discoverer in a dream or vision. Working intensely on a problem and then giving it to God is a proven formula for creative innovation.

We assess our talents, the skills we already have and the skills we need to develop to make it all happen. We stay open to new possibilities even though we have established our beginning course of action.

If we need more training or instruction as we move along, we go out and get it. If our skills need sharpening, we practice them, role-play them with friends or family, do whatever it takes to become professionally adept in whatever we are undertaking.

As we nurture our talents and sharpen our skills, we expand our vistas and our perspective. Pursuing our personal mission is a tremendous opportunity to transcend who we are today to become "who we may be" tomorrow.

Journey in Practical Spirituality: Becoming the Arbiters of Our Destiny

I view the pursuit of mission as a journey in practical spirituality. As we choose to take that journey, we accept the challenge of becoming the arbiters of our destiny.

Thus, each morning before we start our workday, we ask for guidance from our spiritual mentors. We repeat our mission statement out loud as we hold our treasure map before us or envision it in our mind's eye. As we do this, we reinforce the matrix for success in our superconscious, conscious, subconscious and unconscious mind.[5] Thus, even when we are not thinking about our mission per se, we continue to generate creative energy to make it happen from all levels of consciousness.

It is vitally important to our success to live the personal values and principles we have chosen to espouse. This is often easier said than done. It's a stretch to live by our highest values and principles, particularly when they differ from those around us.

How do we do it? By choosing to take the high road even when it's tough to do. We remind ourselves that when we are true to the highest and best in ourselves and true to our God, we are on the right track. We love ourselves through the rough spots and go to our Higher Self for encouragement and comfort.

Fulfilling a Mission is Like Building a Dream House

Let's say your mission is to write books and you envision yourself as a published author whose books make a genuine contribution to people's lives. You want your books to be in line with your values and principles. You also hope to offer inspiration, ideas, information and motivation on subjects that other people need in order to fulfill their mission. (You might guess that this mission is pretty close to home for me!)

Perhaps your goal is one book a year, which means completing two chapters a month for a period of six months, allowing the rest of the year for editing and publishing. A beginning strategy might be to allow the first two weeks of each month for research and creative free-flow writing and the second two weeks to refine those creative bursts into finished chapters.

You would be well advised to take the weekends off—after all, you are embarking on a yearlong project. This is only the beginning, because once you finish the book, it is up to you as the author to help sell it through interviews, lectures, media appearances and book signings.

At the end of the first month, check yourself out. How

am I doing? Am I being realistic in what I have set myself to do? Do I have new information that may alter the way I am doing this? Adjust your strategies, goals or plans of action as necessary. Keep your mission ever before you by envisioning your book making a positive difference in people's lives.

Or perhaps your mission is to be successful in an independent small business. Let's say that your initial definition of success is meeting a goal of increasing gross business income by $1,000 each month. Each month you check it out: How am I doing? Have I met my goals for the month? If not, what do I need to adjust to meet them next month? Do I need to set new goals or strategies in light of new information? If so, what will they be? As you continue to envision your business as successful and thriving, you mobilize the positive energy to make it happen.

Fulfilling a mission is like building a dream house. We have a vision of our dream house. We secure the land, draw up the plans, get the financing and set about building it. When it comes to fulfilling our mission, we go through the same process. We envision it, draw up the plans, get the necessary support and set about making it happen.

Once we have decided upon our mission, vision, values and principles, chosen our specific goals and decided on a strategy, we have begun our journey. We have a plan for navigating rough waters and maximizing progress when the waters are smooth. To top it off, we have recourse to the guidance of the angels and our Higher Self. We are on our way!

Exercise: Charting Your Personal Voyage of Life

Take a moment to look within and contemplate your personal voyage of life, to renew your vision of what you desire to accomplish. Try asking yourself and answering the following questions:

1. *What is my mission? Reflect on yourself and your sense of destiny; meditate on your big dreams. Pray and ask for guidance. Write down your thoughts and dreams and the answers you receive from your prayers.*

2. *What is my vision of the fulfillment of my mission? What will my life look like then? What do I envision and choose to accomplish?*

3. *What values do I espouse? What principles and ethics will I uphold in the name of my personal values?*

4. *What are my special gifts and talents? What skills do I need to offer my gifts to others and to apply my talents?*

5. *What are my specific goals for a month, a year, five years from now? Idea: You may wish to put your goals on a treasure map that covers a month, a year, five years or whatever time period you set.*

6. *What is my overall strategy? How will I go about accomplishing the goals I have set for myself while remaining true to my values, my vision and my sense of mission? How will I keep myself motivated when the going gets tough?*

7. *What is my specific action plan to accomplish my goals a month from now, a year from now, five years from now? Suggestion: Leave yourself open to change as your process moves along. Your guidelines are simply that. Strike a balance between your established action plan and your ongoing creative ideas.*

Epilogue

"Be the change you want to see in the world."
—Mahatma Gandhi

Coming full circle to see ourselves in Thomas Cole's *Voyage of Life* paintings, we see that each cycle of life or lifetime represents a new beginning for our soul. Each of us enters life as the infant self, which represents the innocence of our soul's divine nature.

The Childhood of Our Soul

Our guardian angel gently ferries the child into the waters of life, symbolically representing the womb of the mother as well as the emotions. In our state of innocence the waters seem calm, beautiful, quiet—almost a reflection of the heaven world.

As we meditate upon ourself as this holy child, this blessed soul who comes to earth to fulfill a divine destiny, we may remember entering life on earth with a sense of protection, peace, wholeness and wonder. We may remember or envision that blissful state of innocence and sense the eternal protection, the wise direction and loving care of our Father-Mother God represented by the presence of our guardian angel.

Do you, man or woman, know your soul as the holy innocent? Try envisioning yourself as a special soul who has come from God, accompanied by angels from the realms of glory. Imagine your arrival on earth, innocent, expectant, welcoming the opportunity to fulfill your divine destiny.

Take a moment to remember your childhood: What were you like as a little child? What were your special gifts and talents? Have you developed these precious treasures of your soul, or do they lie dormant within you? Remind yourself: *The unique individual you are and are becoming is your greatest treasure.*

Our Soul as a Stalwart Youth

Now envision or remember yourself, whether man or woman, as a youth—brave, stalwart, filled with excitement and magnificent visions of the future. You are eager to start the next leg of the voyage of life on your own. You feel ready and determined to fulfill your God-given destiny. You eagerly wave goodbye to your guardian angel but secretly hope the angel will be there to help if you capsize the boat.

In the artist's depiction, the soul as a youth takes over the steering of the boat, symbolizing leaving behind childhood or the soul's age of innocence and also symbolizing your soul's eagerness to seek and fulfill your divine destiny through your own creative efforts. Your guardian angel bids you Godspeed and remains on shore as you joyfully, yet a bit tremulously, enter the currents of life on your own.

Do you remember the hopes, dreams and plans of your adolescence and young adulthood? If you are a young adult today, you may still be in that wonderful mode of enthusiasm and excited expectation of what life is to bring. Even more to the point—what will you bring to life?

If you are beyond those special years, do you remember the thrill of setting off by yourself on a quest to fulfill a certain mission, a special dream that you envisioned for your life? Do you remember feeling alternately confident and scared, both ready to face whatever was to come and hoping someone would be there to catch you if you were to fall?

You might wish to make a note about the dreams of your youth: the Saint Francis of Assisi, George Washington, Mother Teresa or Madame Curie[1] or other hero or heroine that you inwardly desired to be.

Rites of Passage for the Soul to Attain to True Adeptship

As you gaze upon the man praying in the midst of the rapids, envision yourself as the budding adept. Here your soul, as the mature, courageous one, is riding out the storm, being tossed in the rapids of life. While using whatever skills you have forged in life, your soul is praying to your God and your guardian angel to guide the boat safely through. You know inwardly that you need help from heavenly realms to make it through the rough waters of life.

What do you know about your personal rough waters? How will you best navigate the rapids of change, the hidden shoals of entrenched habits or stubborn rocks of pride or fear or other character traits that might indeed capsize your boat?

Your guardian angel is in the upper atmosphere, watching but not intervening until called into action through your fervent prayers. In your maturity of soul, you get through the rough waters of life by using all of your strength and wit at the same time that you are on your knees before the power of the Almighty One. Your inner attention is prayerfully fastened upon your God. Thus you meet and pass your tests of life on earth, just as saints and sages from ancient to modern times have passed theirs.

Most of us pray for help when we are in dire straits. As it has been said, "There are no atheists in the foxholes." We would do well to make prayer or meditation a daily ritual.

We may ask ourselves: "Is my soul's attention one-pointed toward passing my tests and fulfilling my divine plan? Is my inner ear inclined to the voice of my guardian angel?"

Do you talk to your God? Do you pray as you face the trials, the temptations, the rapid changes and emotional storms of life? Do you implore your Higher Self to help you claim your victory even as you mobilize all of your inner strength, "know-how" and loving determination to navigate the rapids of change?

Old Age: The Time for Adeptship

In the artist's depiction of old age, the soul as the adept has conquered the human self in the arena of time and space, has made it through the voyage of life and is coming Home. The guardian angel is once again guiding the boat as other angels in the clouds above watch and welcome the soul home from the long and arduous journey of life on earth—home to the heaven-world, home to the Father-Mother God from a journey that perhaps has lasted many lifetimes.[2]

As a wise and seasoned adept, you are prayerful and at peace knowing you have fought the good fight and accomplished your sacred mission on earth to the best of your ability. You gratefully approach reunion with your God, the angels and the saints and sages who have gone before you, as you return to the heavenly realms from whence you came.

Victory in This Life and Many Lifetimes

In my inner vision, these stages of our lives represent the earthly trek of the soul—yours and mine: childhood as our state of innocence, youth as the champion of our vision and mission, adulthood as the forging of our destiny, old age as the fruition of lifelong choices and decisions.

Thus we make of our lives what we will. The angels and our Higher Self intervene only at our request. When we are true to ourselves and to our highest vision, we become heroes or heroines, saints, knight champions in our own right. Ultimately we look forward to returning home to the heaven-world and hearing the words of blessing as Jesus heard them, "This is my beloved Son [Daughter] in whom I am well pleased."[3]

We may look to the Great Lights of the ages, avatars, saints and sages who have preceded us and await the victory of our return. We have learned from them as elder brothers and sisters who have left footprints in the sands of time for us to follow.

Every one of these wayshowers made it through the rough waters of trial and temptation by keeping their vision, mind, heart and soul stayed upon their God. They affirmed hope, lived their faith, took wise and loving action, accomplished good works and trusted the guiding hand of their Higher Self and the angels. In this way, great souls of all ages have won their victory. Ours is before us.

It's a wonderful voyage, this voyage of life in the new millennium. One day our guardian angels will be guiding us home to God. As we near the heaven-world, we will see the saints and our friends of light who have gone before us.

In my envisioning of "life after life," self-transcendence will be an ongoing process as we continue to expand in consciousness and attunement with the infinite Mind of God. Only the Infinite One knows who we may ultimately become—we might say that infinity is the limit. Now, that may boggle our human minds. But I sense our souls smiling and shouting, "Sail on! Infinity is our only limit!"

Meditation: On Readiness to Return Home to God

1. *What do I feel I have accomplished for Father-Mother God during my stay on earth?*

2. *What have I accomplished for the children of God on earth?*

3. *What am I doing right now to fulfill my own soul's destiny?*

4. *What do I still desire to accomplish before returning home to God?*

5. *How do I intend to go about it?*

Appendix

Heart-to-Heart with Dr. Barrick—
Questions and Answers*

Q: It's hard for me to keep up with all the changes in my life. I have just moved my family to a new city and started a new job. This kind of change has always been kind of scary for me. It sounds kind of ridiculous, but sometimes I just want everything to go back to the way it was when I was a kid, when all I had to do was follow my parents' and teachers' rules. I want to be there for my family and to be successful in my new job. What's the best way for me to deal with all this? It feels like a lot!

A: You are definitely moving with the winds of change, but it's understandable that you would be more comfortable with what is familiar. You have lots of company—most of us feel that way! Change brings us face-to-face with the unknown and calls us to step beyond our comfort zone. The good news is that hidden in the unknown is an opportunity to grow, to expand and to become more of who you are.

It's true for your family, too. They have the opportunity to reach out and make new friends and to explore the resources of your new community.

So how about letting your fear be a friendly radar signal! Ask your Higher Self to help you muster the courage to face and accept the unknown. Shout out loud to the angels, "Help me! Help me! Help me!" And they will.

Remember, God loves you and will guide you every step of the way when you ask for help. Pray on a regular basis and get used to the process of discovery and adventure. You can expect many adventures on your new journey.

You may stumble over some boulders of karma and cal-

*Adapted from a column originally printed in *Heart to Heart*, a monthly newsletter published by The Summit Lighthouse, Gardiner, Montana. Excerpted with permission.

cified habits. You may make mistakes along the way. Your loving Father-Mother God will forgive you. Simply ask for forgiveness with a penitent heart and let Father-Mother God know how much you love them. Then forgive yourself, chart a new course—and move on!

Choose to see each new cycle with new eyes, new hope, new perspective. Ask yourself, What is the lesson this cycle brings? What is my opportunity? Then take a cue from the saints who have gone before you. Open your heart and give love to everybody, even when you feel kind of awkward. You would be surprised how many people appreciate a thoughtful gesture, a kind word of appreciation, a helping hand.

Imagine you are a little child, with that sense of wonder and joy at the newness of life, walking with your hand in God's hand. Become the youthful warrior filled with hope and vision of divine destiny. Offer the gift of yourself and your heart's love to each endeavor and to each soul you meet along the way.

Practice saying goodbye to the endings of familiar landmarks and ways of doing things and say hello to the new beginnings. Welcome the chaos of change as part of a transformational process—because that's what it is. Claim your own personal values and principles, live by them and become the arbiter of your own destiny!

One final suggestion: Follow the homely advice of a wise grandmother, "When life hands you lemons, just make lemonade!"

Q: When I turn on the news and see all the earth changes, disasters and conflict around the world, I do my prayers but I still feel upset. How can I handle myself better spiritually and psychologically so that I am prepared to handle whatever comes?

A: I believe that each one of us can handle whatever may be coming if we determine to stand on our own two feet at the same time that we hang onto God's hand. Whatever may come, difficult as it may be, God is on our side. So talk to

God, treat God as your best friend and confidant. Choose to offer an open heart and a friendly smile to everyone you meet.

When you do this, you are beginning to empower yourself to become a living, walking embodiment of God's love— as an Aquarian water bearer of divine love to quench the thirst of all you meet. The world is so thirsty for love. Each of us needs to give that love to our friends and to people we work with on the job and essentially in every dimension of our lives. Now, this may seem like a tall order, but it is our destiny in the Aquarian age—for which all the avatars and saints have prepared the way.

As individuals and as souls, we have been taught the lessons of the preceding ages of Taurus, Aries and Pisces. We understand obedience to God, the importance of knowing ourselves as spiritual seekers and of honing our inner strength. All of this has prepared us for the age of Aquarius where we are meant to fulfill our destiny to offer our gifts to the earth and to one another. We do all this under the direction of our Higher Self, Buddha Self or Christ Self.

In the Buddhic tradition, we are offered the gift of non-attachment to desires and trained to honor the Guru-chela relationship that ultimately we might *realize our own soul's bonding to our Buddha Self.* In the tradition of Abraham and Moses, we have learned a reverence and obedience to the laws of God that we might *know right from wrong within our own hearts.* For the fulfillment of the mission of our Lord and Savior Jesus Christ, we have been shown the path of *tempering the Law by the Spirit of Love.*

As we put these spiritual truths into daily practice, our souls bond more and more with our Higher Self, esoterically known as our Holy Christ Self; we greet difficult experiences with the grace of enlightened understanding.

Set the sail of your consciousness by communing with God in prayer, meditation and the use of the science of the spoken Word (spoken prayer). Put on the Mind of Christ by internalizing the teachings and parables of Jesus. Seek to be true to the laws of God given by Abraham and Moses. Sit under the Bodhi Tree with the Buddha as you study and embrace the Four Noble Truths and the Eightfold Path.[1]

Cultivate loving feelings by recognizing and appreciating God's beauty in people, nature, music, literature and art. Choose to be true to yourself and your God and to behave lovingly—even when you don't feel like it.

Gradually, through daily spiritual practice and God's grace, you will be able to greet life's challenges with empowerment, wisdom and compassion. Ultimately, as you rise in consciousness, you may claim the mantle of an Aquarian Love Conqueror and fulfill your unique mission for Saint Germain, Master of the Aquarian age.[2]

Try this exercise in divine love: Center yourself in the love of your heart. Envision the joy of taking an active role in your family or community according to your special gifts and talents. Image yourself practicing forbearance and learning from someone with whom you disagree. See yourself speaking the truth with kindness, saying an encouraging word and offering a helping hand to family, friends, neighbors, acquaintances and people in the workplace. Now go out and do what you have envisioned—one step at a time!

———————

Q: There seem to be so many problems in my life right now that it's hard for me to keep my faith. What's the best way to get through these difficult times?

A: Such times, when we have so many problems we don't know which way to turn, definitely try our faith. Yet this is often when we reach the greatest heights of self-mastery. So, problems are not necessarily a "problem"—it's a matter of perspective.

Remember that wonderful painting of George Washington kneeling beside his horse at Valley Forge. The artist captured the posture of the striving soul, saint who is committed to action and demonstrates his trust in God and the angels by bending his knee in prayer.

Thus have saints and heroes throughout history made it

through rough times by keeping their vision, mind and heart stayed on God while they took decisive action. So have the ascended masters won their victory. Ours is before us.

If you want to strengthen your faith, "acting as if" will give you a good start. Act as if you had your faith intact, as if God were at your side. The truth is that God *is* right here with you. God will bless you with what you really need anytime you sincerely ask for it.

Hopefully you are saying to yourself, "Okay, I'll try it." Because the inner spiritual meaning of "TRY" is "Theos (God) Rules You."[3] So you have put God in charge, and that's an excellent beginning.

What's next? The overall principle is to pray as if everything depends upon God and take action as if everything depends on you. Here is a seven-step formula:

1. Make a list of your problems. Write them down in order of importance.
2. Decide which problems you can do something about and which ones you haven't a clue how to approach. As you are sorting this out, it's helpful to give the serenity prayer, "Please, God, grant me the courage to change the things I can, to accept the things I cannot change, and the wisdom to know the difference."[4]
3. Next, give the problems you can't change to God. Make a new list of the ones you can do something about. It's a great idea to put the problems you are giving to God on a prayer list that you keep on your altar and to pray to your favorite saint to intercede for you.
4. Now ask your Higher Self, your favorite saint and the angels to help you solve problem number one on your new list.
5. Center in your heart, calm any disturbed emotions through deep, slow breathing, and let your heart tell you how to approach the problem.
6. Set up a specific positive action plan.
7. Do it! And repeat steps 4–7 for every problem on your list.

Notes

Introduction

Opening Quotation: Anonymous.

1. Thomas Cole, *Voyage of Life* (Washington, D.C.: National Gallery of Art, 1842).

Chapter 1: *Forging Our Destiny in a Changing World*

Opening Quotation: John C. Maxwell, *Living at the Next Level: Insights for Reaching Your Dreams* (Nashville, Tennessee: Thomas Nelson Publishers, 1996), p. 100.

1. Patricia Kirmond, *Messages from Heaven: Amazing Insights on Life After Death, Life's Purpose and Earth's Future* (Gardiner, Montana: Summit University Press, 1999).

2. Thornton Wilder, *The Bridge of San Luis Rey* (New York: HarperCollins Publishers, Harper Perennial, 1998), p. 123.

3. Malcolm Muggeridge, modern-day skeptic who became literally transformed by Mother Teresa's presence, wrote a classic account of her journey of compassion: *Something Beautiful for God: Mother Teresa of Calcutta* (New York: Harper & Row, 1986).

4. Licia Corbella, "Small Woman Left Big Impression," *The Calgary Sunday Sun*, December 1, 1996.

5. Elizabeth Clare Prophet with Patricia R. Spadaro and Murray L. Steinman, *Saint Germain's Prophecy for the New Millennium* (Gardiner, Montana: Summit University Press, 1999).

6. Doc Lew Childre, *Cut Thru: Achieve Total Security and Maximum Energy, A Scientifically Proven Insight on How to Care Without Becoming a Victim* (Boulder Creek, California: Planetary Publications, 1996), pp. 70–71. Also see Sara Paddison, *The Hidden Power of the Heart: Achieving Balance and Fulfillment in a Stressful World* (Boulder Creek, California: Planetary Publications, 1995), pp. 59–69.

7. Doc Lew Childre, *Freeze Frame: A Scientifically Proven Technique* (Boulder Creek, California: Planetary Publications, 1997), pp. 38–45.

8. Paul Pearsall, Ph.D., *The Heart's Code: Tapping the Wisdom and Power of Our Heart Energy* (New York: Bantam Doubleday Dell Publishing Group, Inc., Broadway Books, 1998), pp. 99–121.

9. Ibid., pp. 94–97.

10. Ibid., Introduction, pp. 7–8.

11. Ibid., p. 228.

12. Adapted from HeartMath as taught by the Institute of HeartMath in Boulder Creek, California.

Chapter 2: *Exploring the Sacred Miracle of Adeptship*
Opening quotation: Lao-tzu, *The Way of Lao-tzu, I, 33,* trans. Wing-Tsit Chan.

1. See Raymond J. Corsini and Alan J. Auerbach, *Concise Encyclopedia of Psychology,* 2d ed., abr. (New York: John Wiley and Sons, 1998) pp. 861–863.

2. Ibid., pp. 670–671.

3. Laura Lee, foreword to *Awakening to Zero Point: The Collective Initiation,* by Gregg Braden, rev. ed. (Bellevue, Washington: Radio Bookstore Press, 1997), p. viii.

4. Braden, *Awakening to Zero Point,* pp. 145–163.

5. Kuthumi and Djwal Kul, *The Human Aura: How to Activate and Energize Your Aura and Chakras* (Gardiner, Montana: Summit University Press, 1996), pp. 344–45. Also see Pearsall, *The Heart's Code,* pp. 38–61.

6. Hans Jenny, Swiss doctor and scientist, devised specialized apparatus to vibrate sound through various media, thus capturing on film the harmonic and often beautiful patterns produced by sound. Photographs of his sound-created patterns appear in his book *Cymatics* (Switzerland: Basilius Press AG, 1974).

7. Braden, *Awakening to Zero Point,* pp. 21–28.

8. Sara Paddison, *The Hidden Power of the Heart,* pp. 59–69.

9. For a full explanation of the science of prayer, mantras and decrees, see Mark L. Prophet and Elizabeth Clare Prophet, *The Science of the Spoken Word* (Gardiner, Montana: Summit University Press, 1993).

10. Annice Booth, *The Path to the Ascension: Rediscovering Life's Ultimate Purpose* (Gardiner, Montana: Summit University Press, 1999), pp. 198–213. Also see C. W. Leadbeater, *The Masters and the Path* (Kila, Montana: Kessinger Publishing Company, n.d.), pp. 188–209. Originally published by the Theosophical Society.

11. "I am the light of the world: he that followeth me shall not walk in darkness, but shall have the light of life." John 8:12. All Bible verses are from the King James Version unless otherwise indicated.

12. Matt. 5:14–16.

Chapter 3: *Awakening the Gifts of Our Inner Hero*

Opening quotation: James Baldwin, *Everybody's Protest Novel* (1949) and *Notes of a Native Son* (1955).

1. For an excellent and interesting presentation of Carl Jung's archetype of the Shadow, see Connie Zweig, Ph.D. and Steve Wolf, Ph.D., *Romancing the Shadow: Illuminating the Dark Side of the Soul* (New York: Ballantine Books, 1997).

2. The popular Walt Disney movie *Pinocchio* forms the basis of my analysis in this chapter. Carlo Collodi's original nineteenth-century fairy tale *The Adventures of Pinocchio* differs from the movie; however, the basic elements and moral of the story remain the same. The classical story is available in a new translation by Ann Lawson Lucas as a World's Classics paperback (Oxford and New York: Oxford University Press, 1996).

3. Geppetto's wish in the Walt Disney movie *Pinocchio*, 1940; also in Disney's *Pinocchio* (Los Angeles: Disney Enterprises, Inc., Mouse Works Classic Storybook Collection, 1989), p. 8.

4. "When You Wish Upon a Star," concluding song in the movie *Pinocchio*; musical score by Leigh Harline, lyrics by Ned Washington (Los Angeles: Walt Disney Productions, 1940).

Chapter 4: *Shift of the Ages: Light! the Alchemical Key*

Opening quotation: Oliver Goldsmith, *The Captivity, An Oratorio*, Act II (1764).

1. Braden, *Awakening to Zero Point*, pp. 1–56.

2. Laura Lee, foreword to *Awakening to Zero Point*, by Braden, pp. v–viii; pp. 32–40.

3. Mark L. Prophet and Elizabeth Clare Prophet, *Saint Germain On Alchemy: Formulas for Self-Transformation* (Gardiner, Montana: Summit University Press, 1993), p. 49.

4. Braden, *Awakening to Zero Point*, pp. 146–147.

5. Victor Frankl, *Man's Search for Meaning*, rev. ed. (New York: Simon and Schuster, Inc., Washington Square Press, 1985). First published in Austria in 1946 under the title *Ein Psycholog erlebt das Konzentrationslager*.

6. "For who hath known the mind of the Lord, that he may instruct him? But we have the mind of Christ." I Cor. 2:16. Also, "Let this mind be in you, which was also in Christ Jesus." Phil. 2:5.

7. For a beautiful presentation of the story of twin souls, see Elizabeth Clare Prophet, *Soul Mates and Twin Flames: The Spiritual Dimension of Love and Relationships* (Gardiner, Montana: Summit Univer-

sity Press, 1999). Also see Marilyn C. Barrick, Ph.D., *Sacred Psychology of Love: The Quest for Relationships That Unite Heart and Soul* (Gardiner, Montana: Summit University Press, 1999).

8. Mal. 3:2.

9. The "Bodhi tree" was a fig tree (Ficus religiosa), popularly known as a pipal. This tree of enlightenment became an important pilgrimage site for students of the Buddha.

10. Mara is an Eastern personification of Evil; the name means "death." He is likened unto the devil in Christian theology, which is understood esoterically as "deified evil."

11. Karen Yang LeBeau, introduction to Elizabeth Clare Prophet's book *Quietly Comes the Buddha: Awakening Your Inner Buddha Nature* (Gardiner, Montana: Summit University Press, 1998), pp. xxix–xxx.

Chapter 5: *Chaos as Prelude to Personal Metamorphosis*

Opening Quotation: Thomas Carlyle, *On Heroes, Hero Worship and the Heroic in History* (1841).

1. Margaret Wheatley, *Leadership and the New Science: Learning about Organization from an Orderly Universe* (San Francisco: Berrett-Koehler Publishers, Inc., 1994), pp. 121–137.

2. George V. Coyne, "Reflections from a Religious Tradition on the Evolution of Intelligent Life in the Universe" (lecture presented at the Reuben H. Fleet Science Center, University of California, San Diego, California, October 27, 1999).

3. See the video, *Leadership and the New Science*, by Margaret Wheatley, available from CRM Films. For information, call 1-800-421-0833.

4. Wheatley, *Leadership and the New Science*, pp. 101–119; 139–147.

5. Eccl. 3:1–2.

6. Kuan Yin is known in the East as the Goddess of Mercy, who also personifies the Buddhic qualities of invincible wisdom and compassion. She is often depicted gracefully riding a sea dragon over tumultuous waves in a standing posture of complete beauty and serenity.

Chapter 6: *The Odyssey of Self-Transformation*

Opening quotation: Walt Whitman, *Leaves of Grass* (1855–1892), *Aboard at a Ship's Helm*.

1. Homer (c. 700 B.C.), *The Odyssey*, trans. W. H. D. Rouse (New York: A Mentor Book, 1966), pp. 67–70. Some of the spiritual interpretations have been inspired by the unpublished work of Elizabeth Clare Prophet on the tests and initiations of Odysseus, presented at Summit University

in San Diego, California, July 1997.

2. Exod. 21: 24.

3. Homer, *The Odyssey,* p. 107.

4. Ibid., p. 113.

5. Ibid., p. 119.

6. Ibid., p. 140.

7. Ibid., p. 147.

8. Ibid., p. 271.

9. Barrick, *Sacred Psychology of Love,* and Prophet, *Soul Mates and Twin Flames.*

Chapter 7: *Soul Lessons: The Quest of Our Inner Heroine*

Opening quotation: From "Somewhere Over the Rainbow," sung by Judy Garland as Dorothy in the movie *The Wizard of Oz;* musical score by Harold Arlen, lyrics by Yip Harburg.

1. My analysis in this chapter is based on the movie version of L. Frank Baum's modern fairy tale.

2. The concept of the inner girl child as an archetype is explained in the Inner Family Model developed by Caroline C. Hanstke and Brian Grey. This innovative model of the inner self conceptualizes the loving and unloving sides of the archetypes of the inner father, mother, boy child and girl child and how they interact as an inner family. Hanstke and Grey report that the understanding of the dynamics of the inner family facilitates personal transformation and interpersonal effectiveness. For further information on their unpublished manuscript, *Inner Family Workbook,* contact Sirius Consulting Company, 1430 6A NW, Calgary AB, T2M 3G7, Canada or e-mail: Siriusco@cadvision.com.

3. Unity School of Christianity, *Metaphysical Bible Dictionary* (Unity Village, Missouri, 1931), pp. 215–16.

Chapter 8: *The Inner Journey of Endings and Beginnings*

Opening quotation: Robert Browning, *Life in a Love* (1855), stanza 2.

1. From William Wordsworth's timeless poem, *Ode. Intimations of Immortality from Recollections of Early Childhood* (1807), stanza 5:

> "Not in utter forgetfulness,
>   And not in utter nakedness,
> But trailing clouds of glory do we come
>   From God, who is our home."

2. Wheatley, *Leadership and the New Science,* pp. 75–137.

3. Carl Jung and M. L. von Franz, Joseph L. Henderson, Jolande Jacobi, Aniela Jaffé, *Man and His Symbols* (Garden City, New York: Doubleday, 1969), pp. 99, 158–229.

4. Wheatley, *Leadership and the New Science,* p. 103, quoting Deepak Chopra from *The New Physics of Healing* audiocassette (Boulder, Colorado: Sounds True Recording, 1990).

Chapter 9: *Cycles of Change: Beyond the Comfort Zone*

Opening quotation: Jean de La Fontaine, *Fables* (1668), bk VI, fable 5.

Chapter 10: *Transformational Stages of Grief and Renewal*

Opening Quotation: Samuel Daniel, *Sonnets to Delia* (1592), *Sonnet: I Must Not Grieve.*

1. Kahlil Gibran, *The Prophet,* "On Joy and Sorrow" (New York: Alfred K. Knopf, 1923), p. 29.

2. Andrew Auw, *Gentle Roads to Survival: Making Self-Healing Choices in Difficult Circumstances* (Boulder Creek, California: Aslan Publishing, 1991), p. 74.

Chapter 11: *The Gift of Living Fully in the Present*

Opening quotation: *Psalm* 118:24.

1. Djwal Kul, as recorded by Elizabeth Clare Prophet, December 28, 1996, Gardiner, Montana (unpublished).

2. Norman Vincent Peale, *The Power of Positive Thinking* (Englewood Cliffs, New Jersey, Prentice-Hall, Inc., 1952). Also see Napoleon Hill, *Think and Grow Rich! With Peace of Mind,* rev. ed. (New York: Ballantine Books, 1960).

3. From the Walt Disney movie *Bambi,* 1942.

4. Piero Ferrucci, *What We May Be: Techniques for Psychological and Spiritual Growth* (Los Angeles: J. P. Tarcher, Inc., 1982), p. 47.

Chapter 12: *The Alchemy of Self-Transcendence*

Opening Quotation: Eccl. 2:16

1. The "threefold flame" is the divine spark, the flame of God ensconced within the secret chamber of the heart, the soul's point of contact with the Supreme Source. See Prophet and Prophet, *Saint Germain On Alchemy,* p. 455.

2. Barrick, *Sacred Psychology of Love*, and Prophet, *Soul Mates and Twin Flames*.

3. Laurie Beth Jones, *The Path: Creating Your Mission Statement for Work and for Life* (New York: Hyperion, 1996).

4. Thomas á Kempis, *The Imitation of Christ*, rev. trans. (New York: Grossett and Dunlap, Family Inspirational Library, 1973), p. 36.

5. The superconscious is the domain of the Higher Mind from which we receive higher vision, intuition and inspiration. The conscious mind is comprised of the thoughts we are aware of at any given moment. The subconscious is that part of our mind just beyond conscious awareness; thus, we say, colloquially, "It's just on the tip of my tongue." The unconscious is the "hidden" portion of our mind that contains memories, wishes and impulses not directly accessible to our conscious awareness.

Epilogue

Opening Quotation: Mahatma Gandhi as quoted in Rob Gilbert, Ph.D., *Bits and Pieces*, vol. R. no. 5. (Fairfield, New Jersey: Economics Press, Inc., n.d.).

1. Saint Francis of Assisi (1181–1286) was born to wealth, yet devoted his life to poverty. He was concerned for the poor and sick and was a true friend of God's kingdom of nature. George Washington, first president of the United States and commanding general of the American army in the Revolutionary War, was known as the Father of His Country. Mother Teresa of Calcutta, founder of the Missionaries of Charity, was revered by young and old for her selfless, compassionate service to the "poorest of the poor" and was a recipient of the Nobel Peace Prize. Madame Marie Curie, first major female scientist of modern times, discovered radium and won the Nobel Prize in both physics and chemistry.

2. Many of my clients remember past life experiences; the doctrine of reincarnation is a part of some of the world's major religions. My personal experience and belief is that we live many lifetimes until we remember and reclaim our true identity as sons and daughters of God and fulfill our sacred mission on earth.

3. Matt. 3:17.

Appendix: *Heart-to-Heart with Dr. Barrick—Questions and Answers*

1. The Four Noble Truths of the Buddha are 1) Life is pain (suffering); 2) Pain arises from cravings (inordinate desires); 3) Cessation of pain comes through forsaking or nonattachment to cravings; 4) The way of nonattachment is the Noble Eightfold Way (Path), namely, right views (under-

standing), right intention, right speech, right action, right livelihood, right effort, right mindfulness, right contemplation.

See Burtt, editor, introduction and notes, *The Teachings of the Compassionate Buddha* (New York: New American Library, Mentor Religious Classic, 1955) pp. 28–31. Also see LeBeau, introduction to *Quietly Comes the Buddha*, by Prophet, pp. xxix–xxx.

2. See Prophet, Spadaro and Steinman, *Saint Germain's Prophecy for the New Millennium*, pp. 229–292. In this dramatic bestseller the authors tell us that the Comte de Saint Germain was known as the Wonderman of Europe at the end of the eighteenth century when the old order in France was coming to an end. Although the count's birth, death and true identity were shrouded in mystery, he was greatly admired as a philosopher, diplomat, scientist, healer, artist and musician.

As an alchemist and Eastern adept, he amazed the aristocracy and courts of Europe while his true intention was to attempt a smooth transition from the monarchy to a new form of government. He was attempting to establish a united community of Europe in the very face of the impending French Revolution. Today, as an ascended master, Saint Germain comes to the fore as the Master of Freedom and sponsor of the Aquarian age as a new opportunity for a golden-age civilization on earth.

3. "In the word 'try' is the sacred formula of being: Theos = God; Rule = Law; You = Being; Theos + Rule + You = *God's Law Active as Principle Within Your Being (TRY)*." Mark L. Prophet and Elizabeth Clare Prophet, *The Science of the Spoken Word*, p. 104.

4. The "Serenity Prayer" was originally written for Alcoholics Anonymous, by Dr. Bob and Bill W., founders of the nationally recognized self-help support group.

Acknowledgments

I offer this book with the gratitude of my heart and soul to my loving mentors Kuthumi, Jesus Christ, Mother Mary and Saint Germain and all the saints and sages of East and West whose dedication to love and freedom have set the stage for the Aquarian age. I am forever grateful to Mark and Elizabeth Prophet for their delivery of the teachings of the ascended masters who have guided my soul through cycles of change and transformation—and the writing of this book.

I appreciate all the wonderful people who gave time and expertise to assist in the publishing of this book: Roxanne Duke for her magnificent artwork for the cover; Carla McAuley for her excellent ideas and suggestions; Lynda Springer for her skillful copy editing; Kate Doll for her creative flair and expertise in designing and formatting; Nigel and Patricia Yorwerth, Judith Younger, Jeanne House, Janet Lossick, Chris and Marie Antoinette Kelley and Therese Emmanuel for their most helpful input; Norman Millman for his work in foreign rights and distribution; Hertha Lund for her legal assistance; and Phyllis Blain for her invaluable assistance in obtaining rights and permissions for the Thomas Cole artwork from the National Gallery of Art. A very special thank you to family and friends who have loved and cheered me on through the entire process!

Bibliography

Auw, Andrew. *Gentle Roads to Survival: Making Self-Healing Choices in Difficult Circumstances*. Boulder Creek, California: Aslan Publishing, 1991.

Barrick, Marilyn C., Ph.D. *Sacred Psychology of Love: The Quest for Relationships That Unite Heart and Soul*. Gardiner, Montana: Summit University Press, 1999.

Baum, L. Frank. *The Wizard of Oz*. New York: Konecky and Konecky, 1900.

Booth, Annice. *The Path to the Ascension: Rediscovering Life's Ultimate Purpose*. Gardiner, Montana: Summit University Press, 1998.

Braden, Gregg. *Awakening to Zero Point: The Collective Initiation*, rev. ed. Bellevue, Washington: Radio Bookstore Press, 1997.

Brisson, Barbara Schiff. *Such Is the Way of the World: A Journey through Grief*. Mahwah, New Jersey: Paulist Press,1997.

Burtt, E.A., ed., introduction and notes. *The Teachings of the Compassionate Buddha*. New York: New American Library, Mentor Religious Classic, 1955.

Casarjian, Robin. *Forgiveness: A Bold Choice for a Peaceful Heart*. New York: Bantam Books, 1992.

Childre, Doc Lew. *Cut-Thru: Achieve Total Security and Maximum Energy*. Boulder Creek, California: Planetary Publications, 1996.

Childre, Doc Lew. *Freeze Frame: A Scientifically Proven Technique*. Boulder Creek, California: Planetary Publications, 1997.

Collodi, Carlo. *The Adventures of Pinocchio*. Translated by Ann Lawson Lucas. Oxford and New York: Oxford University Press, World's Classics, 1996.

Corsini, Raymond J. and Auerbach, Alan J. *Concise Encyclopedia of Psychology*, 2d. ed., abr. New York: John Wiley and Sons, 1998.

Disney's *Bambi*. Los Angeles: Disney Enterprises, Inc., Mouse Works Storybook Collection, 1942.

Disney's *Pinocchio*. Los Angeles: Disney Enterprises, Inc., Mouse Works Storybook Collection, 1989.

Ferrucci, Piero. *What We May Be: Techniques for Psychological and Spiritual Growth*. Los Angeles: J. P. Tarcher, Inc., 1982.

Frankl, Victor. *Man's Search for Meaning*, rev. ed. New York: Simon and Schuster, Inc., Washington Square Press, 1985.

Gandhi, Mahatma in *Bits and Pieces*, vol. R., no. 47. Edited by Gilbert, Rob, Ph.D. Fairfield, New Jersey: Economics Press, Inc., n.d.

Gibran, Kahlil. *The Prophet*. New York: Alfred K. Knopf, 1923.

Hanstke, Caroline and Grey, Brian, unpublished manuscript, *Inner Family Workbook*, Calgary, Alberta, Canada: Sirius Consulting Company, 2000.

Hill, Napoleon. *Think and Grow Rich! With Peace of Mind*, rev. ed. New York: Ballantine Books, 1960.

Homer. *The Odyssey*. Translated by W. H. D. Rouse. New York: Mentor Book, 1966.

Jenny, Hans. *Cymatics*. Switzerland: Basilius Press AG, 1974.

Jones, Laurie Beth. *The Path: Creating Your Mission Statement for Work and for Life*. New York: Hyperion, 1996.

Jung, Carl and von Franz, M. L., Henderson, Joseph L., Jacobi, Jolande, Jaffé, Aniela. *Man and His Symbols*. New York: Doubleday, 1969.

Kempis, Thomas à. *The Imitation of Christ*, rev. trans. New York: Grossett and Dunlap, Family Inspirational Library, 1973.

Kirmond, Patricia. *Messages from Heaven: Amazing Insights on Life After Death, Life's Purpose and Earth's Future*. Gardiner, Montana: Summit University Press, 1999.

Kuthumi and Djwal Kul. *The Human Aura: How to Activate and Energize Your Aura and Chakras*. Gardiner, Montana: Summit University Press, 1996.

Leadbeater, C. W. *The Masters and the Path*. Kila, Montana: Kessinger Publishing Company, n.d. Originally published by the Theosophical Society.

Maxwell, John C. *Living at the New Level: Insights for Reaching Your Dreams*. Nashville, Tennessee: Thomas Nelson Publishers, 1996.

Mother Teresa. *No Greater Love*. Foreword by Thomas Moore. Novato, California: New World Library, 1997.

Muggeridge, Malcolm. *Something Beautiful for God: Mother Teresa of Calcutta*. New York: Harper & Row Publishers, 1986.

Paddison, Sara. *The Hidden Power of the Heart: Achieving Balance and Fulfillment in a Stressful World*. Boulder Creek, California: Planetary Publications, 1995.

Peale, Norman Vincent. *The Power of Positive Thinking.* Englewood Cliffs, New Jersey: Prentice-Hall, Inc., 1952.

Pearsall, Paul, Ph. D. *The Heart's Code: Tapping the Wisdom and Power of Our Heart Energy.* New York: Bantam Doubleday Dell Publishing Group, Inc., Broadway Books, 1998.

Prophet, Mark L. and Elizabeth Clare. *Saint Germain On Alchemy: Formulas for Self-Transformation.* Gardiner, Montana: Summit University Press, 1993.

Prophet, Mark L. and Elizabeth Clare. *The Science of the Spoken Word.* Gardiner, Montana: Summit University Press, 1993.

Prophet, Elizabeth Clare, with introduction by LeBeau, Karen Yang. *Quietly Comes the Buddha: Awakening Your Inner Buddha Nature.* Gardiner, Montana: Summit University Press, 1998.

Prophet, Elizabeth Clare with Spadaro, Patricia R. and Steinman, Murray, L. *Saint Germain's Prophecy for the New Millennium.* Gardiner, Montana: Summit University Press, 1999.

Prophet, Elizabeth Clare. *Soul Mates and Twin Flames: The Spiritual Dimension of Love and Relationships.* Gardiner, Montana: Summit University Press, 1999.

Salzberg, Sharon, with foreword by Jon Kabat-Zinn. *LovingKindness: The Revolutionary Art of Happiness.* Boston, Massachusetts: Shambhala Publications, Inc., 1995.

Simon, Dr. Sidney B. and Simon, Suzanne. *Forgiveness: How to Make Peace with Your Past and Get On with Your Life.* New York: Warner Books, Inc., 1991.

Unity School of Christianity. *Metaphysical Bible Dictionary.* Unity Village, Missouri, 1931.

Westberg, Granger E. *Good Grief.* Philadelphia, Pennsylvania: Fortress Press, 1982.

Wheatley, Margaret. *Leadership and the New Science: Learning about Organization from an Orderly Universe.* San Francisco: Berrett-Koehler Publishers, Inc., 1994.

Wilder, Thornton. *The Bridge of San Luis Rey.* New York: HarperCollins Publishers, HarperPerennial, 1998.

Zweig, Connie, Ph.D. and Wolf, Steve, Ph.D. *Romancing the Shadow: Illuminating the Dark Side of the Soul.* New York: Ballantine Books, 1997.

Marilyn C. Barrick (1932–2007), Ph.D., minister, psychologist and transformational therapist is the author of a seven-book, self-help series on spiritual psychology: *Sacred Psychology of Love: The Quest for Relationships That Unite Heart and Soul; Sacred Psychology of Change: Life as a Voyage of Transformation; Dreams: Exploring the Secrets of Your Soul; Emotions: Transforming Anger, Fear and Pain; Soul Reflections: Many Lives, Many Journeys; A Spiritual Approach to Parenting: Secrets of Raising the 21st Century Child* and *Everything Is Energy: New Ways to Heal Your Body, Mind, & Spirit.*

The Summit Lighthouse®
63 Summit Way, Gardiner, Montana 59030 USA
1-800-245-5445 / 406-848-9500

Se habla espanol.

TSLinfo@TSL.org
SummitLighthouse.org

www.ingramcontent.com/pod-product-compliance
Lightning Source LLC
Chambersburg PA
CBHW062050270326
41931CB00013B/3021